THE KEIGHLEY AND WORTH VALLEY RAILWAY

HERITAGE RAILWAY GUIDE

THE KEIGHLEY AND WORTH VALLEY RAILWAY

HERITAGE RAILWAY GUIDE

PETER WALLER

PEN & SWORD TRANSPORT

AN IMPRINT OF PEN & SWORD BOOKS LTD.
YORKSHIRE - PHILADELPHIA

The Keighley and Worth Valley Railway

First published in Great Britain in 2023 by
Pen and Sword Transport
An imprint of
Pen & Sword Books Ltd.
Yorkshire - Philadelphia

ISBN 978 1 52670 221 0

Typeset in 11/13 Palatino by SJmagic DESIGN SERVICES, India.

Printed and bound by Printworks Global Ltd, London/Hong Kong.

Pen & Sword Books Ltd incorporates the imprints of Pen & Sword Books Archaeology, Atlas, Aviation,
Battleground, Discovery, Family History, History, Maritime, Military, Naval, Politics, Railways, Select,
Transport, True Crime, Fiction, Frontline Books, Leo Cooper, Praetorian Press, Seaforth Publishing,
Wharncliffe and White Owl.

For a complete list of Pen & Sword titles please contact

PEN & SWORD BOOKS LIMITED
George House, Units 12 & 13, Beevor Street, Off Pontefract Road, Barnsley, South Yorkshire, S71 1HN, England
E-mail: enquiries@pen-and-sword.co.uk
Website: www.pen-and-sword.co.uk

or

PEN AND SWORD BOOKS
1950 Lawrence Rd, Havertown, PA 19083, USA
E-mail: uspen-and-sword@casematepublishers.com
Website: www.penandswordbooks.com

CONTENTS

Acknowledgements and Author's Note 6

Abbreviations 7

Introduction 8

Genesis 9

Grouping to Closure 19

Preservation – The Early Years 29

Consolidation 44

Into the 1980s and beyond 85

The Last Thirty Years 97

Vintage Carriages Trust 114

Bahamas Locomotive Society 116

Lancashire & Yorkshire Railway Trust 117

Bibliography 119

ACKNOWLEDGEMENTS AND AUTHOR'S NOTE

The majority of the images used in this book are drawn from the collections held by the Online Transport Archive. This is a charity devoted to the saving and preservation of primarily transport related illustrative material. Other material has been supplied by my good friends Gavin Morrison, Robin Leleux and, through Andrew Royle, by Transport Treasury.

The decision was made to stop the detailed narrative on the development of the KWVR towards the end of the twentieth century. In my opinion, the most interesting aspects of the history of the line are covered by the periods before it was preserved and in the first quarter century of its life in preservation; there have obviously been changes and improvements in the years since 1990 – such as the enhanced catering facilities at Oxenhope – but many of these developments are building upon the principles and policies established between 1965 and 1990. The Worth Valley is a relatively short line; there is a limit to what can be achieved once all the stations have, for example, been restored. The facilities that the line can offer for locomotive and rolling stock restoration are amongst the best in preservation and the products of these workshops can be seen illustrated throughout this book.

ABBREVIATIONS

BLS	Bahamas Locomotive Society
BP&GV	Burry Port & Gwendaeth Valley
BR	British Rail(ways)
GCR	Great Central Railway
GNR	Great Northern Railway
GWR	Great Western Railway
ICI	Imperial Chemical Industries
KWVR	Keighley & Worth Valley Railway
KWVRPS	Keighley & Worth Valley Railway Preservation Society
LMS	London, Midland & Scottish Railway
LNER	London & North Eastern Railway
LNWR	London & North Western Railway
LRO	Light Railway Order
LYR	Lancashire & Yorkshire Railway
MS&L	Manchester, Sheffield & Lincolnshire Railway
MSC	Manchester Ship Canal
NCB	National Coal Board
NER (BR)	North Eastern Region/North Eastern Railway
NS	Nederlandse Spoorwegen (Dutch State Railways)
NRM	National Railway Museum
RSH	Robert Stephenson & Hawthorns Ltd.
PKP	Polskie Koleje Państwowe (Polish State Railways)
SEC	South Eastern & Chatham Railway
SJ	Statens Järnväger (Swedish State Railways)
SRPS	Scottish Railway Preservation Society
USATC	United States Army Transportation Corps
VCT	Vintage Carriages Trust
WYPTE	West Yorkshire Passenger Transport Executive

INTRODUCTION

It is now more than five decades since the ex-Midland Railway branch line between Keighley and Oxenhope reopened to passenger services as a preserved line. This means that the line has now been in preservation for almost as long as it was operated by the Midland (56 years) and longer than it was operated by both the LMS (25 years) and British Railways (14 years). Over that period, the line has carried many thousands of enthusiasts, day trippers and locals, all of whom are able to savour the experience of travelling up the valley to Oxenhope via the tourist magnet that is represented by Haworth with all its connections to the famous Brontë family.

Going back to the early 1960s, however, it was the closure of another line – the ex-Great Northern route to Bradford or Halifax – that inspired the founding fathers of the Keighley & Worth Valley Preservation Society. It was witnessing the demise of this line that encouraged the pioneers, led by people like the late Bob Cryer, to vow that a similar fate would not befall the branch to Oxenhope once it was clear that British Railways was determined to close the line. Although Beeching and his notorious report 'The Reshaping of Britain's Railways' is often cast as the villain in stories of railway preservation, in the case of the line through the Worth Valley complete closure had already been completed by the date of the report; the demise of the Oxenhope branch was symptomatic of the gradual elimination of the nation's railway network that had been undertaken even before the Beeching 'Axe' was wielded.

Preservation in the early 1960s was still very much in its infancy; the first standard-gauge line to be preserved in Britain — the Middleton Railway — in Leeds had only been secured in 1959 and the campaign to save the first ex-British Railways line – the Sheffield Park to Horsted Keynes line in Sussex – was still in its infancy.

As was often the case with early preservation, many of the ideals that fostered the scheme proved ill-founded; almost from the start the concept of running a commuter service – for which purpose a couple of redundant ex-British Railways railbuses were acquired – proved over optimistic but, since the line reopened in 1968, it has established itself as an important contributor to the local economy and, with the wheel turning full circle, increasingly perceived as forming part of a more integrated transport facility serving this part of the West Riding at a time when roads are becoming more congested.

This, then, is the story of the branch from Keighley to Oxenhope from its origins in the middle of the nineteenth century through to the thriving preserved line of today.

GENESIS

Bradford was 'and is' situated along a valley that runs due south-east from the Aire Valley at Shipley; the most logical means of approach, therefore, historically was along the valley formed by the Bradford Beck and it was this route that the Bradford Canal, a branch off the Leeds-Liverpool, took. The canal opened in 1774 and was to survive until 1922 when it closed. The first railway to serve Bradford, the Leeds & Bradford, also ran through the Aire Valley and was authorised on 4 July 1844. The line opened from Leeds (Wellington) to Bradford (Market Street) on 1 July 1846. To the west of Shipley, the towns of Bingley, Keighley and Skipton were growing and on 30 June 1845 the Leeds & Bradford Railway was authorised to construct an extension from Shipley to Colne, via Skipton, and a west-south curve at Shipley to form a triangle. The line opened from Shipley to Keighley on 16 March 1847, thence to Skipton on 8 September 1847 and the final section, through to Colne, on 2 October 1848.

The Leeds & Bradford Railway was destined to have a short independent existence as, following an Act of 24 July 1851, it was formally invested into the Midland Railway. The Worth Valley, running southwards from Keighley, was also experiencing some growth; partly this was the result of the expansion in the textile industry locally but it was also the result of the growing reputation of the Brontë family, whose home had been in Haworth, aided by the publication in 1857 of Mrs Elizabeth Gaskell's *The Life of Charlotte Brontë*.

The Brontë family had moved to Haworth in April 1820, when Patrick Brontë (1777-1861) was appointed vicar of the local parish church. The family moved into the Parsonage – the home of the Brontë Museum from the late 1920s – from Thornton, near Bradford, where Partrick Brontë had been curate of the church. Brontë and his wife Maria (1783-1821) had six children: Maria and Elizabeth, both of whom died in

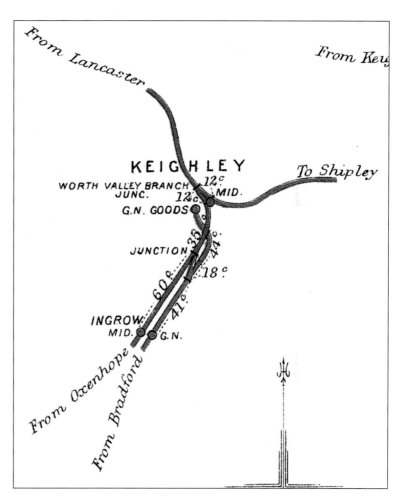

The environs of Keighley station as illustrated in the Railway Clearing House map of the lines in the area in 1913, showing the connection between the Great Northern line to Queensbury and the location of the GNR goods yard in the town, which was accessed by a freight-only spur under the Midland Railway branch.

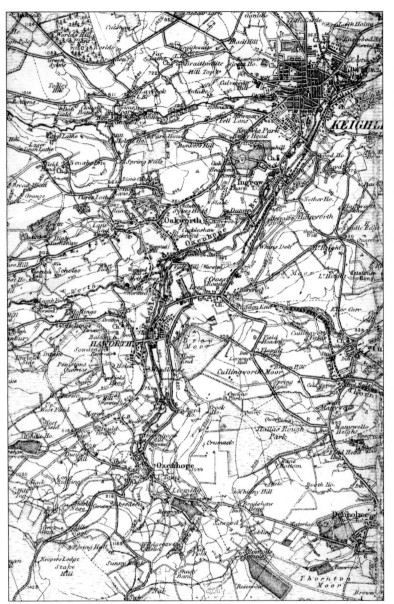

Map of the Oxenhope branch showing the Great Northern Railway route heading in from the east and running parallel to the branch for some considerable distance.

1825, Charlotte (1816-1857), Patrick Branwell (1817-1848), Emily (1818-1848) and Anne (1820-1849). Charlotte, Emily and Anne – under the pseudonyms of Currer, Ellis and Acton Bell respectively – started their literary careers in the late 1840s; Charlotte's best-known work is *Jane Eyre*, first published in 1847; Emily is perhaps best known as the author of *Wuthering Heights*, also published in 1847; Anne's best-known novel is *The Tenant of Wildfell Hall*, which came out in 1848. All of Patrick Brontë's children predeceased him and, after their deaths, he did much to promote their literary name.

One incident towards the end of the 1840s indicated the lack of a railway serving Haworth; in 1848, Charlotte and Anne Brontë travelled to London to reveal the true identities of Currer and Acton Bell. Whilst they were able to travel by train from Keighley to the metropolis, the first part of their journey from Haworth to Keighley had to be accomplished on foot. There had been plans for the construction of a line prior to this date. The 1845 Act permitting the extension of the Leeds & Bradford Railway had authorised a line through the Worth Valley and in October 1845 an alternative line – promoted with the support of Patrick Brontë – called the Manchester, Hebden Bridge & Keighley Junction Railway was also proposed. In the collapse of many railway schemes following the 'Railway Mania' of 1845, these two proposals both failed and it would not be until well after the death of the noted authors that the valley would resonate to the sound of a steam train.

In August 1861, a circular was issued on the subject of a proposed meeting for the construction of a railway to Haworth. Although the original date of the meeting – 13 September 1861 in the Black Bull Inn in Haworth – was missed, a meeting held on 8 October 1861 saw the resolution passed:

That this meeting, being fully convinced that a Railway from Keighley to Haworth is necessary for the maintenance of the present value of property, the general welfare of the Locality and the industrial progress, pledges itself to subscribe and to obtain subscribers for the accomplishment of the object, being convinced that it will form a good investment of capital, and that the question of its prolongation to Lowertown [part of Oxenhope where the actual station was eventually constructed] depends upon its Survey, and probable traffic and subscription.

A second resolution passed saw a number of individuals pledge themselves to take shares in the railway; these included the MP for Keighley, Isaac Holden (who was later knighted), who agreed to subscribe to £2,500 worth of shares. This meeting was followed up by another, again in the Black Bull Inn, at which the civil engineer John MacLandsborough reported that he had surveyed the route through to Oxenhope and had come up with an estimated cost for the work.

Backed by the Midland Railway, the original Keighley & Worth Valley Railway was authorised by an Act of 30 June 1862 to construct a 4¾-mile long branch from Keighley through Haworth to Oxenhope with an average gradient of 1 in 70. The money to build the line was to be raised locally but the Midland agreed to operate the line from its opening. The contract to build the route was given to John Metcalf of Bradford on 19 January 1864 and the first sod was cut by the chairman, Isaac Holden, on 9 February 1864. A price for the supply of the track by the Darlington Iron Co at £7 10s per ton was agreed on 3 January 1865. Construction proceeded apace, although the creation of the 150yd long Ingrow Tunnel resulted in serious subsidence to the newly built Wesley Place Methodist chapel during the spring of 1865; following an official complaint, and after an agreement reached at a meeting held on 5 May 1865, the building had to be dismantled and rebuilt on an adjacent site, although the railway's contention was that

One of the Keighley Tramway Co's horse trams is pictured at the Ingrow Bridge terminus of the first tram route to serve the town. *Barry Cross Collection/Online Transport Archive*

One of Keighley Corporation's twelve double-deck trams stands on the railway bridge adjacent to the station in Keighley. This was one of the original batch of ten trams delivered in 1904; when delivered all ten were open-top, but open-balcony top-covers were fitted to all between 1910 and 1912. *Barry Cross Collection/ Online Transport Archive*

the chapel builders were aware of the location of the tunnel and that the primary cause of the original building's failure was inadequate foundations upon poor quality ground. A further setback, following the contractor running the first engine up the branch to Oxenhope on 1 November 1866 to signal the line's completion, occurred later the same month when, following heavy rain, flooding resulted in 40m of the embankment at Damems being washed away and there was also a landslip at Haworth. Although the line was built with a single track, enough land was acquired to construct all the formation and structures to take a second track if necessary.

Following three years of construction and the necessity of raising additional capital from the shareholders, the line officially opened on 13 April 1867, the actual opening being delayed as a result of the necessity of repairing the line following the flooding of November 1865. Normal passenger services commenced on 15 April 1867 with intermediate stations at Ingrow, Oakworth and Haworth; Damems station – claimed to be Britain's smallest standard-gauge station (station rather than halt as it was originally provided with a stationmaster's house) – opening on 1 September 1867. The initial gradient from Keighley was 1 in 58; this has proved to be a challenge over the years, particularly in wet weather, and a portent for the future occurred when the opening special, formed of a locomotive, guard's van and seven coaches, stalled on the gradient and had to set back into Keighley. It was more successful at the second time of asking, although it stalled for a second time between Oakworth and Haworth. Freight services started on 1 July 1867, with freight facilities provided at all intermediate stations, including a siding at Damems. For the line's first year of operation, services were maintained by the contractors that had built the line.

The line seems to have been a success from the start with the *Keighley News* reporting at the end of May 1865 that:

> Since the Worth Valley Railway was opened it has been the means already of bringing thousands of visitors to the ancient village of Haworth. During the past few Sundays, hundreds have been enjoying the pure air and mountain breezes in the romantic neighbourhood. To all appearances it is very likely to become a general pleasure locality in the summer months.

For a decade, the junction at Keighley was situated on the line from Leeds or Bradford towards the Lancashire coast; the Midland Railway, courtesy of the line through Sedbergh and the London & North Western, could gain access to Carlisle, but the importance of the Aire Valley line increased immeasurably when the Midland took the decision to

One of Keighley Corporation's last batch of trolleybuses – No 15 of 1924 – seen on Skipton Road. The history of trolleybus operation in the town is surprisingly complex for a relatively small system, but the Oxenhope railway faced competition on two fronts: a route from the town centre to Oakworth that opened on 15 December 1914 and a route to Oxenhope via Ingrow. The first section of the latter – to Cross Roads – opened on 3 May 1913 but the extension to Oxenhope, although completed in 1916, did not open until 1921! The Oxenhope extension was shortlived – it was withdrawn on 24 October 1921 and the Oakworth route followed on 2 December of the same year. The last trolleybuses operated in Keighley on 31 August 1932 and on 30 September 1932 the corporation-owned buses that had replaced the trolleybuses were taken over by a new joint venture with the West Yorkshire Road Car Co Ltd – Keighley-West Yorkshire Services. The buses would continue to compete with the railway until the latter's closure. *Barry Cross Collection/Online Transport Archive*

construct its independent main line to Carlisle – the Settle & Carlisle was born, opening to passenger services in April 1876. Keighley station now resounded to the noise of Anglo-Scottish expresses running between Edinburgh and London St Pancras. Between then and the outbreak of the First World War, traffic over the line increased significantly, with the result that the bulk of the route between Leeds and Skipton was quadrupled between 1896 and 1910; the section from Thwaites through Keighley to Snaygill, however, remained double track only.

The Oxenhope branch was leased to the Midland Railway (authorised on 11 August 1876) and five years later, on 1 July 1881, the larger company formally absorbed the line although the original Worth Valley Railway Co was not finally wound up until late in 1886. Under the terms of the Midland Railway (Additional Powers) Act of 1881, the line was acquired for £14,500. In the decade following the Midland's acquisition, concern grew with regards to the timber Vale Mill Viaduct south of Oakworth. In 1891, the railway obtained powers to construct a deviation route. The new route, which included a new stone-built viaduct and the 75yd-long Mytholmes Tunnel, opened on 6 November 1892.

The late nineteenth century witnessed considerable expansion in the railway network as the main line railway companies sought to compete with each other. In the West Riding, one of the most significant companies in competition with the Midland was the Great Northern and one of the battlefields between the two was the triangle formed by

Oxenhope station
pictured during the first decade of the twentieth century.
Real Photographs

Bradford, Keighley and Halifax. Part of the impetus to this development was the failure to construct a link line through the centre of Bradford – a problem still unresolved to this day – and both the Midland and Great Northern railways had plans for the construction of lines via Queensbury linking the three towns. In the event, it was the Great Northern that came out victorious, but the construction of its line was a long drawn out affair. Originally empowered by an Act of 5 August 1873 to construct a line from Thornton to Keighley, it was not until 1 September 1882 that a single-track line was opened from Thornton to Denholme for goods services; passenger services over the line to Denholme commenced on 1 January 1884. The line was extended through to Keighley for freight on 1 April 1884. Great Northern passenger services were extended to Ingrow on 7 April 1884 and to Keighley itself on 1 November 1884.

Although originally the GNR had planned to construct its own station in Keighley, following an agreement of 1 June 1881 it was agreed between the two railways that the GNR would share accommodation in a relocated station in Keighley. When the Leeds & Bradford Railway had originally opened its line west from Shipley, Keighley station was situated to the west of a level crossing serving Bradford Road. The new station was to be sited to the east of Bradford Road, where a road overbridge replaced the level crossing, at the junction with the branch to Oxenhope. The new station was to have four platforms – two on the main line and two serving the Oxenhope branch and the GNR services to Halifax and Bradford. As part of the development, the Midland Railway doubled the line between Keighley and the junction with the spur that provided a link through to the GN lines. The site of the old Keighley station was used to provide a vastly enlarged goods yard whilst the GNR had separate goods facilities located to the west of the Worth Valley line; these were accessed by a double-track line that passed under the Worth Valley line between Ingrow and Keighley stations. In addition, the GNR constructed a shed at Ingrow to house its locomotives. The new station at Keighley opened on 6 May 1883.

Haworth station seen during the first decade of the twentieth century. The station as portrayed here was the result of enlargement in 1900. The work at the time also included the removal of a footbridge at the country end of the platform and the replacement of the goods shed with a much larger structure. In the distance a service towards Oxenhope can be seen approaching the station. *Real Photographs*

Keighley station 'as rebuilt in 1883' is pictured in circa 1905; these platforms are these that served the main line between Shipley and Skipton and the view is towards Skipton. *Real Photographs*

The next transport development towards Ingrow came later in the same decade when, on 8 May 1889, the 4ft 0in gauge horse trams of the Keighley Tramways Co Ltd started to operate on the route from North Street, about ¼-mile from the station, to Ingrow. The route was extended from Keighley to Utley on 18 December 1889. The arrival of the tram marked the effective end of the railway's monopoly of public transport in the area. The 2¼-mile long route was never a financial success; indeed, the company only ever paid a dividend when it was wound up following sale to Keighley Corporation in 1901, the latter having obtained powers to take over and electrify the route in 1898. When sold, the company's thirty horses and six tramcars raised a total of £804. Keighley Corporation took over in September 1901 and continued to operate a horse-tram service until May 1904 and a new electric tramway was introduced in October the same year. Electric services operated also over a branch from North Street, via the station, to Victoria Park; this route was extended in February 1905 to serve Stockbridge.

Like many railways, the Oxenhope branch was largely constructed to accommodate double track if the traffic warranted such a provision; the branch as completed, however, was single track throughout and the lack of passing loops was a further severe constriction on increasing traffic. As a result, loops were installed at both Haworth and Oakworth to permit trains to cross; these were both brought into use during April 1900. In terms of signalling, the branch had effectively been operated as a single section controlled by a train staff. The opening of the loops resulted in the introduction of the electronic train tablet system between Keighley and Haworth although the section between there and Oxenhope retained traditional staff working.

Although there were proposals to extend the tramways further, these failed to progress as the corporation decided to invest in a new form of transport — the trolleybus. From 1913, three routes were introduced using the unusual Austrian-supplied Cedes-Stoll system; these ran from Utley to Sutton-in-Craven, from The Cross to Oakworth and, most significantly from the Midland Railway's standpoint, from Ingrow initially to Cross Roads with an extension to Oxenhope being completed in 1916 (but due to the First World War, not opening until 1921). The use of Austrian-made equipment meant that there was a problem in obtaining spares during and after the war with the result that by the date the Oxenhope extension opened, the Cedes-Stoll trolleybuses were already proving unreliable and inadequate; in fact the Oxenhope extension lasted only until October 1921. In principle (but hardly in practice), for the first time, the Oxenhope branch had a direct competitor.

In 1923, the Corporation decided to replace its electric trams and remaining Cedes-Stoll trolleybuses with a more conventional trolleybus system. However, the Ingrow-Cross

The well-kept station at Ingrow pictured in a view taken circa 1905 looking towards Keighley. Today the view is very different as Ingrow is home to the Vintage Carriages Trust, the *Bahamas* Locomotive Society and the station itself is different; the original station was demolished and the ex-MR station from Foulridge, on the closed Skipton to Colne line, rebuilt in its place. *Real Photographs*

KEIGHLEY and OXENHOPE.—Midland.

(Down and Up timetable, Week Days and Sundays — Midland Railway)

Down — stations:
- 610 Leeds .... dep.
- 610 Bradford (Mkt. St.)
- 613 Skipton
- Keighley .... dep.
- Ingrow
- Damems
- Oakworth
- Haworth
- Oxenhope .... arr.

Up — stations:
- Oxenhope .... dep.
- Haworth
- Oakworth
- Damems
- Ingrow [613]
- Keighley ‡ 381, 610, arr.
- 610 Skipton .... arr.
- 613 Bradford (Mkt. St.)
- 613 Leeds (Wellington)

a. Arrives at 6 28 aft. on Saturdays.	k. Arrives at 3 17 aft. on Saturdays.
e. Except Saturdays.	l. Arrives at 10 23 aft. on Saturdays.
n. Runs 5 minutes later on Saturdays.	s. Saturdays only.
x. Arrives at 6 31 aft. on Saturdays.	y. Leaves at 11 10 aft. on Saturdays.
‡ Station for Worth Valley.	

Keighley and Oxenhope

The Oxenhope branch timetable for April 1910.

Roads Cedes-Stoll trolleybuses soldiered on until May 1926; the electric trams to Ingrow were replaced by new trolleybuses in December 1924 – this was the last of Keighley's tram routes to operate, with the routes to Utley and Stockbridge having succumbed in August and November 1924 respectively. The Corporation continued to operate trolleybuses until August 1932 when they were replaced by buses; initially these were Corporation owned but were later to form part of a joint operation with the West Yorkshire Road Car Co.

In the pre-Grouping era, the MR generally employed 0-6-0Ts on the branch. These included five – Nos 218, 219, 1397-99 – that were built at Derby (Order No 414) in 1883; these were modified Johnson '1102' class locomotives that were fitted with fully-enclosed cabs. All were rebuilt in 1901 and further modified in 1910. In 1907 the quintet became Nos 1725-29 respectively. Post-Grouping, Nos 1725/27-29 received replacement Belpaire G5 boilers between 1924 and 1928 but Nos 1728 and 1729 were not to last much longer, being withdrawn in December 1932 and July 1931 respectively. The remaining three survived to pass into BR ownership. No 41725 was withdrawn in August 1955, No 41727 in March 1952 and the last – which was only fitted with a second-hand replacement G5 boiler in 1950 – was No 41726, which was not withdrawn until July 1959. By the BR era, however, their connection with the Worth Valley was long over; in 1950, No 41725 was allocated to Shrewsbury, No 41726 to Derby and No 41727 to Gloucester. A further batch of five locomotives – Nos 1111-15 – were also designed eventually for operation on the branch; constructed at Derby (Order No 991), these locomotives were fitted with half-cabs. Modified in January 1910, having been renumbered 1820-24 in 1907, the five received replacement G5 boilers between 1926 and 1928. Four of the five – Nos 1820-23 – were withdrawn in the early 1930s, although No 1820 was reinstated in 1933; this locomotive 'along with No 1824' survived to pass into BR ownership. No 41820 – allocated to Skipton in 1950 – and 41824 – to Swansea Victoria – were withdrawn in August 1952 and January 1951 respectively.

By 1923, the railway to Oxenhope was under new management. As a result of the Grouping of the railways in January of that year, the Midland Railway had ceased to be and a new railway – the London, Midland & Scottish – had been created to take over the Midland's assets along with those of a number of other pre-Grouping companies; Keighley station was, however, still to resound to the locomotives of two railway companies as the Great Northern line towards Bradford and Halifax had passed to the rival London & North Eastern.

GROUPING TO CLOSURE

The interwar period witnessed few changes other than that of ownership. There was a great variation in terms of locomotives used, with 0-6-0 tender locomotives appearing and 0-4-4Ts being utilised on push-pull services. The timetable for August 1939 – the last before the outbreak of the Second World War – saw fifteen return workings per day along the branch with sixteen on Saturdays; the Sunday service was six return workings. The wartime years and the immediate post-war period saw a considerable reduction in the level of service. The last LMS timetable issued in 1947 noted that there were nine return workings on weekdays, twelve on Saturdays and four on Sundays. Perhaps more pertinently, except on Saturdays, there were no services departing from Oxenhope on weekdays between 8.20am and 1.50pm and none from Keighley between 8am and 1.15pm. The gap in service was even more pronounced on Sundays, with no Down services from Keighley before 5.20pm and no Up services to Keighley before 5.40pm. In an era when people had increasing amounts of leisure time and the private car was becoming more common, the lack of earlier Sunday services can almost be guaranteed to have forced people to use other means of transport for days out. Another rationalisation was the closure of Damems station on 23 May 1949. By this date, the LMS had been nationalised and operation of the branch now fell to the London Midland Region of British Railways.

Passenger services over the ex-Great Northern route to Queensbury were withdrawn on 23 May 1955. The lines were to remain open for freight traffic following closure but the section between Cullingworth and Ingrow East was to close completely on 28 May 1956. The ex-GNR Keighley South goods yard – by now accessed from the

The LMS service over the Oxenhope branch as recorded in the August 1939 edition of *Bradshaw's Guide. Author's collection*

KEIGHLEY and OXENHOPE timetable (Bradshaw's Guide, August 1939)

First class Privilege ticket valid from Damems. *Author's collection*

LMS era third-class ticket from Oakworth to Keighley. The dating is imprecise but would appear to be 9 August 1941. *Author's collection*

ex-Midland line – was closed on 17 July 1961 and the final section of the ex-GN network in Keighley – the short section from the station to Ingrow East – closed completely on 28 June 1965.

Alongside the closure of the ex-GNR route, there was also some rationalisation along the Oxenhope branch. The signal boxes were closed and the signalling dismantled in late 1955; for the remainder of its life under BR, the branch was operated on the 'one engine in steam' principle, controlled from Keighley GN Junction box. Ground-frames were installed at Haworth and Oakworth; these were operated by the crossing-keepers at the two stations. With the closure of the booking offices – tickets were latterly sold on board the trains – the crossing-keepers became the only full-time staff employed specifically

Timetable for services between Keighley and Oxenhope from the LMS timetable for the period from 16 June to 5 October 1947. *Author's collection*

Table 258 — KEIGHLEY and OXENHOPE

Week Days

Mls. from Keighley	Station	p.m	a.m	p.m	a.m S	p.m S	p.m S	p.m E	p.m S	a.m
	209London (St. Pan.). dep	9 30	..	11B50	..	..	..	..	..	9 55
	Keighley .... dep	6a10	6 53	8a 0	9 15	1210	1 5	1 15	1 50	4p 5
1¼	Ingrow	6 14	6 57	8 4	9 19	1214	1 9	1 19	1 54	4 9
2¼	Damems		7 0	8 7		1217	1 12	1 22	1 57	4 12
2¾	Oakworth	6 19	7 3	8 10	9 24	1220	1 15	1 25	2 0	4 15
3½	Haworth............	6 23	7 7	8 14	9 28	1224	1 19	1 29	2 4	4 19
4¾	Oxenhope .... arr	6 26	7 10	8 17	9 31	1227	1 22	1 32	2 7	4 22

Week Days—Continued. / **Sundays**

Station	p.m	a.m	a.m	p.m	a.m	a.m	p.m	p.m
209London (St. Pan.) dep	..	11E50	11S50	12S55	10 15	11 50	2 50	..
Keighley .... dep	4 50	5p37	6p22	8 45	5p20	6p30	7 30	9 10
Ingrow	4 54	5 41	6 26	8 49	5 24	6 34	7 34	9 14
Damems	4 57	5 44	6 29		5 29	6 39	7 39	9 19
Oakworth	5 0	5 47	6 32	8 54	5 29	6 39	7 39	9 19
Haworth............	5 4	5 51	6 36	8 58	5 33	6 43	7 43	9 23
Oxenhope .... arr	5 7	5 54	6 39	9 1	5 36	6 46	7 46	9 26

Week Days

Miles	Station	a.m	a.m	a.m	a.m S	p.m S	p.m S	p.m E	p.m	p.m
—	Oxenhope .... dep	6 33	7 13	8 20	9 40	12 30	1 30	1 50	2 12	4 25
1¼	Haworth............	6 36	7 16	8 23	9 43	12 33	1 33	1 53	2 15	4 28
2	Oakworth	6 39	7 19	8 26	9 46	12 36	1 36	1 56	2 18	4 31
2½	Damems	6 42	7 22	8 29		12 39		1 59	2 21	4 34
3¼	Ingrow.............	6 45	7 25	8 32	9 51	12 42	1 41	2 2	2 24	4 37
4¾	Keighley .... arr	6 48	7 28	8 35	9 54	12 45	1 44	2 5	2 27	4 40
219¼	209London (St.Pan.). arr	12p25	1p55	2p25	4p 0	7 10	..	9 0	9 0	..

Week Days—Continued. / **Sundays**

Station	p.m	p.m	p.m	p.m	p.m	p.m	p.m	p.m
Oxenhope .... dep	5 15	5 57	6 42	9 5	5 40	7 0	8 0	9 30
Haworth............	5 18	6 0	6 45	9 8	5 43	7 3	8 3	9 33
Oakworth	5 21	6 3	6 48	9 11	5 46	7 6	8 6	9 36
Damems	5 24							
Ingrow.............	5 27	6 8	6 53	9 16	5 51	7 11	8 11	9 41
Keighley .... arr	5 30	6 11	6 56	9 19	5 54	7 14	8 14	9 44
209London (St.Pan.) arr	..	..	5H15	5F30	..	..	4K40	7K25

a a.m. **B** Except Saturday and Sunday nights. **F or E** Except Saturdays. **F** Except Sundays mornings.
H Sunday mornings only. **K** Monday mornings. *p* p.m. **S or S** Saturdays only.

On 3 August 1947, five months before the line passed to the newly created British Railways, Johnson Class 1P 0-4-4T No 1361 stands at Oxenhope station with the 5.40pm service to Keighley. *W.A. Camwell/SLS Collection*

The same service is seen at Keighley following its arrival. No 1361 was coming towards the end of its life by this date. It was withdrawn for scrap in February 1948. *W.A. Camwell/ SLS Collection*

Recorded in 1949, shortly before its closure, Damems station originally opened on 1 September 1867. The station, with its one-coach length platform, was the smallest on the MR. It was opened to serve a small mill and limited freight facilities were provided until 23 May 1949. After closure, the small station buildings were demolished but have been recreated post-preservation. Although smaller than many halts, Damems was technically a station as there was a stationmaster; the original stationmaster's house is still extant. The level crossing to the south of the station was worked by a ground frame that was located in the garden of the stationmaster's house; the last crossing keeper, employed since 1928, was Annie Feather, who lived in the house. *Transport Treasury*

on the branch. In later years, the steam passenger service saw Ivatt-designed 2-6-2Ts supplant the older ex-MR 0-4-4Ts. The remaining freight traffic was generally hauled by Class 3F 0-6-0s.

In the 1950s, British Railways rationalised its regional boundaries; the original boundaries had been based upon the companies from which the lines had been inherited but now a much more rational approach was taken. The result was that the Oxenhope branch along with the main line passed to the North Eastern Region from the London Midland. The new owners, however, did not foresee a long-term future for the line and in July 1959 issued a notice of closure subject to approval by the local Transport Users Consultative Committee. The latter rejected BR's efforts to close the line, suggesting that the costs of operating the branch could be reduced and that services would be enhanced by the introduction of modern diesel units. The introduction of such stock elsewhere – much cleaner than the steam trains replaced – had resulted in significant increases in passenger traffic and, it was hoped, the combination of economies plus additional passenger revenue would improve the branch's economics. BR took action and the new diesel units were introduced to the line on 13 June 1960. The final timetable for the branch

On 30 July 1951 ex-LMS Class 1P 0-4-4T No 58075 approaches Ingrow West at 6.30pm with a service from Keighley to Oxenhope. *Tony Wickens/Online Transport Archive*

The same train as seen in the previous photograph pictured at Oxenhope station at 6.40pm. The quiet of the station platform is in stark contrast to the scene on today's preserved railway. *Tony Wickens/Online Transport Archive*

Pictured at Keighley, ex-LNER Class N1 0-6-2T No 69464 departs with a service towards Queensbury at 7.10pm on 30 July 1951. It is interesting to note that graffiti was a problem even then! *Tony Wickens/ Online Transport Archive*

Second class ticket from Oakworth to Haworth dated 30 March 1959. *Author's collection*

On **15 August** 1959, an afternoon service for Oxenhope enters Ingrow station headed by Ivatt 2-6-2T No 41326. *Gavin Morrison*

showed fifteen return workings per weekday with an additional five return workings on Saturdays; there was still, however, no Sunday service.

The efforts that the NER took to improve the line's finances were, however, probably too little and too late. A further application to withdraw the service was made and this time, despite much opposition, the Transport Users Consultative Committee agreed to BR's proposals. The final passenger services operated on Saturday 30 December 1961. The final timetable, covering the period from September 1961 to June 1962, saw a supplement issued in December 1961. Comments therein included, 'The Passenger Train has been withdrawn from Ingrow, Oakworth, Haworth and Oxenhope. *Delete* this table.' The supplement also recommended passengers use the parallel buses operated by West Yorkshire; after almost 80 years, road transport had proved victorious. This was not quite the end of the branch, as freight services continued to operate from Great Northern Junction at Keighley to Oxenhope until 18 June 1962. The very last train to operate over the line was a special organised by the newly-established Keighley & Worth Valley Railway Preservation Society that ran on 23 June 1962 headed by Class 3F 0-6-0 No 43586.

There the story might have ended but for the determination of a band of enthusiasts who were determined to see that the ex-Midland Railway branch did not go the same way as the ex-GNR routes had done the previous decade.

On 29 August
1959, Manningham-allocated Ivatt Class 2MT No 41326 is seen in platform 3 at Keighley station awaiting departure with a service to Oxenhope. New in April 1952, when the locomotive was allocated to Skipton, No 41326 was transferred to Manningham during the early summer of 1957. *Alec Swain/ Transport Treasury*

As the last of the passengers from the train makes her way off the platform, No 41326 is pictured again, this time after completing the journey to Oxenhope. No 41326 was to remain based in Bradford for four years, before a final transfer saw it move to the Southern Region, where it was allocated to Brighton for the remainder of its career. It was finally withdrawn in May 1964. *Alec Swain/Transport Treasury*

Indicative perhaps of the station staff's estimation of the number of potential passengers is the extent of the platform at Oxenhope that hasn't been cleared of snow as Fairburn-designed 2-6-4T No 42139 shunts its two-coach train prior to running round. *Henry Priestley/Transport Treasury*

KEIGHLEY TO OXENHOPE — WEEKDAYS (DOWN) — H 48

All trains marked **B**, **Diesel**, **2 L62**.

Mileage M C	Station																							
						SO	SO			SO	SX	SO										SO	SO
0 0	KEIGHLEY dep	6 50	7 40	9 15	10 0	10 42	11 40	12 20	1 5	1 15	1 50	2 40	3 45	4 25	5 17	5 57	6 37	7 34	8 14	9 12	10 33	11 15
1 15	Ingrow	6 54	7 44	9 19	10 4	10 46	11 44	12 24	1 9	1 19	1 54	2 44	3 49	4 29	5 21	6 1	6 41	7 38	8 18	9 16	10 37	11 19
2 54	Oakworth	6 59	7 49	9 24	10 9	10 51	11 49	12 29	1 14	1 24	1 59	2 49	3 54	4 34	5 26	6 6	6 46	7 43	8 23	9 21	10 42	11 24
3 42	Haworth	7 3	7 53	9 28	10 13	10 55	11 53	12 33	1 18	1 28	2 3	2 53	3 58	4 38	5 30	6 10	6 50	7 47	8 27	9 25	10 46	11 28
4 62	OXENHOPE arr	7 6	7 56	9 31	10 16	10 58	11 56	12 36	1 21	1 31	2 6	2 56	4 1	4 41	5 33	6 13	6 53	7 50	8 30	9 28	10 49	11 31

OXENHOPE TO KEIGHLEY — WEEKDAYS (UP)

All trains marked **B**, **Diesel**, **2 L62** except last column **C**, **Emerg Diesel Units**, **3 L62**.

Mileage M C	Station																						
				SO	SO			SO	SX	SO											SO	SO
0 0	OXENHOPE dep	7 10	8 10	9 35	10 21	11 5	12 0	12 40	1 30	1 45	2 10	4 5	4 52	5 40	6 17	7 0	7 55	8 35	9 30	10 51	11 35
1 20	Haworth	7 13	8 13	9 38	10 24	11 8	12 3	12 43	1 33	1 48	2 13	4 8	4 55	5 43	6 20	7 3	7 58	8 38	9 34	10 54	11 40
2 8	Oakworth	7 16	8 16	9 41	10 27	11 11	12 6	12 46	1 36	1 51	2 16	4 11	4 58	5 46	6 23	7 6	8 1	8 41	9 37	10 57	11 43
3 47	Ingrow	7 21	8 21	9 46	10 32	11 16	12 11	12 51	1 41	1 56	2 21	4 16	5 3	5 48	6 28	7 8	8 6	8 46	9 43	11 2	11 50
4 62	KEIGHLEY arr	7 24	8 24	9 49	10 35	11 19	12 14	12 54	1 44	1 59	2 24	4 19	5 6	5 51	6 31	7 11	8 9	8 49	9 46	11 6	11 53

Issued by the North Eastern Region, this was the branch-line timetable for the period from 11 September 1961 through to 17 June 1962. By this date, the services had been dieselised with a single journey taking 16min from Keighley to Oxenhope on average and 14min in the reverse direction. This was the last timetable to record a BR service on the line as services ceased on 31 December 1961. *Author's collection*

On 23 June 1962, some six months after the line had lost its passenger services and a week after freight services were withdrawn, the Keighley & Worth Valley Railway Preservation Society organised a special from Bradford Forster Square hauled by Manningham-allocated Class 3 0-6-0 No 43586 to mark the line's final closure. Here is the view at Oxenhope station with the locomotive having run round the train before heading back towards Keighley tender first. By this date, the locomotive was also approaching the end of its operational life; having been based at Manningham since late 1955, it was finally withdrawn on 2 August 1962. *Yorkshire Post/Transport Treasury*

PRESERVATION – THE EARLY YEARS

T he tourist potential of the line had been demonstrated as far back as 18 May 1895 when the Midland Railway operated a special train to Haworth to mark the opening of the new Brontë Museum, but it was the creation of the preservation society that gave an impetus to the line's survival. The process of preservation was, however, destined to be a long one. Although the concept of railway preservation had been established by the early 1960s – as evinced by the Talyllyn, Ffestiniog and Middleton railways – the idea of taking over closed BR lines had only just been realised

Pictured at Whitsun 1965 in the yard at Haworth in its unrestored form is the ex-MS&LR four-wheel tricomposite coach now owned by the Vintage Carriages Trust. The coach, built at the railway's works at Gorton in 1876, was to become GCR No 176 following the renaming of the railway in 1897. It survived to become part of the BR departmental fleet, serving as a tool and stores van (No DE953003), until it was acquired for preservation in 1961. Limited conservation work was undertaken but serious restoration was not started until 1983, with work being completed two years later. The coach had originally one first class, one second class and two third class compartments with a central compartment to store luggage. With the abolition of second class, this compartment was made first class (although there was no physical upgrade of the facilities – thus the restored coach has two first class compartments: one very plush that was the original first class and one with leather seating that would have been second class originally). *Phil Tatt/Online Transport Archive*

The Horsham-based Chipman Chemical Co had first supplied weed-killing equipment and chemicals to the Southern Railway before the Second World War and post-nationalisation this commercial relationship continued. In the mid-1950s, the company's involvement with the railway industry expanded with a train being equipped for use by the Eastern and North Eastern regions; a further two trains were also in service by the early 1960s and one of these included an ex-GNR bogied milk van (No 4151) as No CWT3. Although it is suggested that the train in which No CWT3 operated was withdrawn in 1966 with the van being preserved on the KWVR the following year, its presence in the yard at Haworth at Whitsun 1965 would suggest that the train was taken out of service earlier. Sadly, the van was subsequently scrapped. *Phil Tatt/Online Transport Archive*

with the opening of the Bluebell Railway from Sheffield Park to Bluebell Halt in 1960; the line was extended into Horsted Keynes two years later.

Shortly before the final closure of the line, a local resident, Ralph Povey, wrote a letter to the *Telegraph & Argus* in Bradford; in this he advocated that local residents act to preserve the line. This led – on 24 January 1962 – to a public meeting being held in the Keighley Temperance Hall; this was organised by Bob Cryer and the enthusiasm that the meeting engendered led to a series of further meetings and on 1 March 1962 to the formation of the Keighley & Worth Valley Railway Preservation Society. Two months later, the society took on the lease of Haworth station – for £65 per annum plus rates – and on 23 June 1962 organised the special hauled by No 43586. With a base established at Haworth, locomotives and rolling stock started to arrive and Haworth station was opened on Sundays to allow visitors to inspect progress.

Following two years of negotiation, it was announced at a meeting on 22 September 1964 that BR had agreed to sell the line to the KWVRPS and that the society hoped to introduce weekend services in June 1965 with the intention of introducing a weekday commuter service soon thereafter. The society's chairman – Bob Cryer – commented that he hoped that half of the 300,000 passengers that had used the line prior to closure annually would make use of the new service. The purchase price – quoted as 'some thousands of pounds' – was to be spread over several years. To facilitate the line's purchase, the Keighley & Worth Valley Light Railway Ltd was formally incorporated on 8 February 1966. In 1968 it was reported that the purchase price from BR was a payment of £3,500 per annum for twenty-five years for the entire branch with the exception of the last 100 yards into platform 4 at Keighley, where BR retained ownership but leased the section to the company. There was no interest charged on the outstanding sum nor was there any increase in the price over the years; the railway paid off the final instalment in 1992.

As was often the case in preservation, this early optimism had to be revised in the light of experience. The first locomotive to arrive on the line was ex-LYR No 51218, which was delivered on 7 January 1965. It was not until 6 March 1965 that the first train to operate over

Pictured in the yard at Haworth on 29 September 1965 is ex-LYR 'Pug' No 51218; this was the first locomotive to arrive on the KWVR in January of that year. The locomotive was used prior to the line's formal reopening for the movement of empty stock from Keighley to Haworth. Built at Horwich in October 1901, No 51218 was one of twenty-three of the design to pass into BR ownership in 1948 and, not being withdrawn until September 1964, was the last of the type to remain on the main line. Latterly based at Neath in South Wales, No 51218 was purchased for preservation. Last operated in 2006, No 51218 is currently on static display at Oxenhope although there are plans for its eventual restoration to steam. *Charles Firminger/Bob Bridger Collection/Online Transport Archive*

The station at Haworth recorded on 29 September 1965. *Charles Firminger/Bob Bridger Collection/Online Transport Archive*

the line since June 1962 ran. Following track work – which had seen some 1,500 rotten or missing chairs replaced by members of the society – the preserved ex-GNR 'J52' 0-6-0T No 1247, then owned by Captain W.G. Smith and which had arrived on the line in March 1965, operated two services from Keighley to Haworth to deliver stock, the first departing at 2.30pm. The stock delivered included two locomotives – the Gresley Society's ex-GNR Class N2 0-6-2T No 69523 (as LNER No 4744) and the restored ex-LYR Barton Wright-designed 0-6-0 No 957 – as well as a number of carriages. The new arrivals joined ex-LYR 'Pug' 0-4-0ST No 51218 and the Manning Wardle 0-6-0ST *Sir Berkeley*, which had both been delivered by road and which were already in residence in the goods shed at Haworth. With the coaches – built originally for the MS&L, GN and SEC railways – stored on the adjacent sidings, members of the preservation society progressed with the work of track and rolling stock restoration.

On 31 July 1965, No 51218 hauled one of the railway's carriages – an ex-Southern Railway 'Matchboard' third-class coach (No 3554) – out of the shed at Haworth, repainted into the primrose and dark blue livery that the railway initially intended to adopt. The carriage was then attached to 'N2' No 4744 to convey a working party to Keighley where the train was coupled up to a further stock delivery; this comprised an ex-LNER

Gresley-designed BSK No E16250, an ex-MR 54ft clerestory coach at the time numbered in the departmental series DM195955M, and three ex-Metropolitan Railway carriages. The last three, plus the ex-Southern carriage, had originally been preserved for the proposed preservation of the Westerham branch in Kent but had been transferred to Keighley following the failure of that scheme. The three ex-Metropolitan carriages – brake third No 427, third class No 465 and first class No 509 – were also planned to receive the primrose and blue livery.

As work on the restoration of the line continued, further rolling stock was delivered. On 19 March 1966, No 51218 made a further trip to Keighley, this time returning to Haworth with a further two carriages. These were a Gresley-designed buffet – No NE1852E – that dated originally to 1938 and an ex-LYR directors' saloon – No Sc45038M – that was built in 1878 but which had been latterly based at Wick. One of the consequences of the use of No 51218 on work such as this over the steeply graded branch was that it was fitted with a vacuum brake to enable it to operate works trains.

During the summer of 1967, the first intimations of a return of passenger trains to the branch were advertisements that appeared in the local press announcing that the railway intended to apply to the Ministry of Transport for a Light Railway Order for the line. The application was to be made in the name of the British Railways Board and, should the

Viewed from the level crossing to the west of the station, the track through Oakworth was weed strewn and rusting when pictured here in September 1965; it was to be almost another three years before services were restored over the line. The view shows the remains of the goods loop in the level crossing; this loop, which had a trailing connection into the goods yard, was lifted by British Railways in the late 1950s. Although it features on large scale Ordnance Survey maps as late as 1969, photographs exist that show its removal by 1960. *Charles Firminger/Bob Bridger Collection/Online Transport Archive*

It is four years after closure and, although the track and buildings at Oxenhope remain intact, there is an air of decay about the scene; weeds are growing through the track and there are piles of detritus on the platform. Only two years later, the empty platform would resound once again to trains and crowds as the line reopened. *R.C. Riley/ Transport Treasury*

LRO be granted, a further order would be sought to transfer the LRO to the Keighley & Worth Valley Light Railway Limited. At the time, it was hoped that the process would permit services to be restored in August 1967, but this was to be unduly optimistic.

Although full services were not yet operational, 13 April 1967 saw the railway celebrate the centenary of the line's opening in 1867 by the operation of a special works train – with appropriate celebratory headboard – from Keighley; this was hauled by the ex-NER Class J72 No 69023 – by now named *Joem* – assisted at the rear by Ivatt-designed 2-6-2T No 41241. As the line's opening got closer, further locomotives and rolling stock continued to arrive, such as the ex-Manchester Ship Canal 0-6-0T No 31 *Hamburg*, which had been built by Hudswell Clarke in 1903 and which arrived on the railway on 17 June 1967. A later arrival that year, having been purchased from the scrap line at Salisbury by a member of the society in August 1967, was 'USA' 0-6-0T No 30072. During the course of 1967, a total of some 31,000 people visited the museum at Haworth, an encouraging number as the prospect of restored services grew closer. Work to make the railway operational continued; this included the installation of a water tower at Oxenhope and the acquisition of machine tools to help make the shed at Haworth into a functioning workshop.

When it was first proposed that the line be preserved, one of the intentions was to operate a daily commuter service; whilst in reality this never proved practical, in late 1967 two items of rolling stock were delivered that could have delivered such a service. These

Prior to the line's reopening, the yard at Haworth was a draw to locals and enthusiasts and a number of events were held. In May 1966 the crowds have gathered to examine the rolling stock that had already arrived on the line. Visible locomotives include ex-GNR 0-6-0T No 1247 and 0-6-2T No 4744. *Phil Tatt/Online Transport Archive*

were two of the four-wheel diesel railbuses that BR had acquired in the late 1950s in the hope of reversing the declining fortunes of some of the more rural branch lines. Amongst the units that BR acquired were five manufactured by the German company Waggon und Maschinenbau and fitted with Büssing 150bhp engines. New in 1958 and allocated to the Eastern Region, Nos E79960-64 were all withdrawn between November 1966 and April 1967. The railway acquired two of the batch – Nos E79962 (still fitted with its original Büssing engine) and E79964 (fitted with a replacement AEC unit) – and the pair arrived on the line in November 1967. Although never destined to operate a commuter service, the pair were employed on passenger services; for example, the winter service operated from November 1970 saw a diesel-only service on Saturdays with limited steam operation on Sundays.

Prior to the formal opening of the line, the railway was used during late March and early April 1968 by the BBC for the recording of a television series based upon the classic

One of the facets of an event held in May 1966 was the operation of a shuttle powered by ex-LYR 'Pug' No 51218 from the goods shed in Haworth yard to the end of the loop. Coaching stock was provided by ex-Southern Brake Third No 3554. Although designed by Maunsell for the South Eastern & Chatham Railway, the 'Matchboard' coach was built post-Grouping at the Birmingham-based Metropolitan Carriage, Wagon & Finance Co in July 1924 (to Diagram 164A). Designed for use on boat train traffic to and from the harbours at Dover and Folkestone, the carriage was initially preserved following withdrawal in July 1961 for a planned – but unsuccessful – attempt to preserve the Westerham branch in Kent. Reaching Keighley by rail in January 1965, it was transferred to Haworth on 6 March 1965. The coach was acquired in 1972 by the VCT – the railway having acquired more modern rolling stock – for restoration; it is currently restored to its BR guise as No S3554S in carmine and cream livery. *Phil Tatt/Online Transport Archive*

book *The Railway Children* by E.E. Nesbitt; this was to be the precursor for the filming of the classic Lionel Jeffries' version a few years later. The series was first broadcast starting on 12 May 1968. In May 2021, the filming for a sequel to the 1970 film – *The Railway Children Return* – commenced in Haworth; the film was released during the summer of 2022 (sadly without the critical acclaim that the original engendered).

In the summer of 1968 it was announced that the Ministry of Transport inspection of the line was to take place on 8 June; assuming that the inspector gave the go-ahead, it was hoped to launch the first passenger services on 29 June with the first departure from Keighley being at 2.35pm. The proposed return fares were 10s (50p) adult and 5s (25p) children. Come the appointed day, crowds gathered to witness the line's reopening as the first service – double-headed by Ivatt No 41241 in maroon (a non-authentic livery that

Pictured at Leeds Holbeck shed in April 1967, ex-MR 0-6-0T No 41708 had been purchased by the Midland Railway Locomotive Fund, a group established in 1964, during 1966. Built at Derby in 1880 as No 1418, the locomotive was renumbered 1708 in 1927. Although rebuilt with a Belpaire firebox in 1927, the locomotive retained its half cab. Fitted with air brakes in 1940, No 1708 was requisitioned by the military during the Second World War and was used on the Melbourne Military Railway in Derbyshire between April that year and December 1944. Its final operational allocation was to Barrow Hill shed where it was used for shunting at the Staveley Ironworks. These duties ceased with dieselisation in 1965 and when finally withdrawn in 1966 No 41708 was the oldest operational locomotive on BR. One of the last five of the class to survive, No 41708 was selected for preservation as being in the best condition. Used intermittently on the KWVR from April 1971, the locomotive departed the railway in 1974 initially to Butterley. The locomotive has been based at – appropriately – Barrow Hill for almost two decades at the time of writing and in June 2019 ownership passed from the Midland Railway Locomotive Fund to the Barrow Hill Engine Shed Society. Work on restoring the locomotive, which was last steamed in 2003, commenced in late 2020. *John Worley/Online Transport Archive*

the locomotive was to retain until it was restored to BR black in 1980) and 'USA' tank No (300)72 in a brown and black livery – departed from a heavily decorated platform 4 at Keighley station. The six-coach train comprised two of the ex-Metropolitan Railway carriages, one ex-Southern, one ex-LMS and two Pullman cars; these were first-class *Zena* and second-class *Lorna*. The launch of the service was undertaken by the then Mayor and Mayoress of Keighley – Alderman and Mrs J.H. Waterworth – and representatives from BR, who had been involved in the process of the line's preservation, were also present.

Pictured in the yard at Haworth in April 1967 is rebuilt 'Royal Scot' No 46115 *Scots Guardsman*. As LMS No 6115 the locomotive was originally built by North British in Glasgow during 1927 and was named the following year. Rebuilt to William Stanier's design in 1947 and fitted with smoke deflectors – the only rebuilt 'Royal Scot' to be so equipped prior to nationalisation – No 46115 spent much of its post-1948 career based at either Crewe or one of the Carlisle sheds (Upperby or Kingmoor). Preserved by the late Bob Bill on withdrawal in January 1966, the locomotive is portrayed here still bearing the yellow cab-side stripe that indicated that it was barred from operating south of Crewe over the 25kV West Coast main line. A heavy locomotive and thus unsuitable, at the time, for operation over the Worth Valley, No 46115 was transferred to the Dinting Railway Centre in May 1969. *John Worley/Online Transport Archive*

On arrival at Oxenhope, the train was greeted by a brass band playing *Congratulations!* Ironically, although services were operational on the branch, there were no train services on British Rail: this was due to industrial action, part of a work-to-rule campaign.

The line was legally operated by the Keighley & Worth Valley Light Railway Ltd on behalf of the preservation society. The deal with BR meant that, for the first time, a group was to operate a preserved railway into an operational BR station. Initially services were limited to Saturdays and Bank Holidays – with seven return workings per day – and Sundays with five. Fares for the return trip were 4s (20p) adult and 2s (10p) for children. The majority of services were timetabled for steam haulage with diesels potentially in use for the last return workings on Sundays.

Purchased by the Gresley Society in October 1963 following withdrawal in September 1962 and initially stored at Harworth Colliery, No 4744 was transferred to the Worth Valley on loan in 1965 and is seen in the yard at Haworth in April 1967. The locomotive – the only surviving example of a Gresley-designed Class N2 0-6-2T – was one of a class of 107 constructed between 1920 and 1929. Built at North British in February 1921 as GNR No 1744, the locomotive became LNER 4744 at Grouping and was renumbered 9523 under the post-war LNER renumbering scheme. Whilst on the Worth Valley, the locomotive was amongst those featured during the filming of *The Railway Children*. Unfortunately, the locomotive did little work on the line thereafter as a result of a boiler tube failure. No 4744 was transferred to Quorn & Woodhouse, on the preserved Great Central, in November 1975 where the extensive boiler work required to restore the locomotive to working order was undertaken. *John Worley/Online Transport Archive*

Another ex-GNR locomotive based at Haworth for a brief period was Captain Bill Smith's Class J52 0-6-0T No 1247. Built to the design of Henry Ivatt, No 1247 was built at Sharp, Stewart & Co in Glasgow during May 1899. Becoming LNER No 4247 at Grouping and No 8846 following the post-war renumbering, it ended its career as BR No 68846 based at King's Cross from where it was withdrawn in May 1959. Purchased on withdrawal – the first locomotive to be acquired directly for preservation from BR by a private individual – No 1247 was based on the Bluebell Railway until 1965 when it was transferred to the Worth Valley. It remained on the line until 1970 when it was moved to the Birmingham Railway Museum at Tyseley. *John Worley/Online Transport Archive*

Above: **Between 1900** and 1923, almost 100 'Dreadnought' carriages were constructed for the Metropolitan Railway; the last survivors remained in service until September 1961 and the electrification of the Amersham line. Six coaches were then retained by London Transport until May 1963 for use in the centenary of the opening of the first stretch of the future Underground network. Three of these were purchased by David Kitton for use on the proposed preserved Westerham branch; this scheme, however, failed and the coaches were placed on loan to the KWVR in July 1965. Here one of the trio – seven-compartment Brake Third No 427 (with a body built in 1910 on an underframe that was five years older) – is seen in the yard at Haworth in April 1967 having been repainted into the blue and primrose livery that the KWVR adopted initially. No 427 along with another 'Dreadnought' – No 465 – were used as part of the reopening train in June 1968. The three ex-Metropolitan coaches were purchased by the VCT in 1974. The carriage has spent most of its career on the KWVR in authentic liveries, but it reverted temporarily in 2008 to the livery illustrated here to mark the 50th anniversary of the line's reopening. *John Worley/Online Transport Archive*

Opposite above: **Following its** withdrawal from Skipton shed, to which it had been reallocated from Llandudno Junction in August 1965, in December 1966, Ivatt 2-6-2T No 41241 made its way under its own steam to Keighley in early 1967. It is seen here at Haworth in July that year in 'as withdrawn' condition, prior to being repainted by the railway into the maroon livery. *Phil Tatt/Online Transport Archive*

Opposite below: **There are** few locomotive designs that can claim to have been constructed over more than half a century, but the Wilson Worsdell-designed 0-6-0T (designated Class J72 by the LNER) was one. A total of eighty-five were constructed between 1898 and 1925 but a further twenty-eight were built, largely without any serious modification to the original design, for BR between 1949 and 1951. Two of the BR-built batch – including No 69023 of April 1951 – were transferred to departmental stock in October 1964 and following withdrawal No 69023 was preserved by R. Ainsworth in September 1966. It was moved to the KWVR in September 1966 and is pictured here at Haworth in July 1967 having been named *Joem* in tribute to the owner's parents (Joseph and Emily). It was destined to be based on the KWVR for a relatively brief period and was transferred to the Derwent Valley Light Railway near York when that railway started summer passenger services in 1977. These services ceased, however, in 1979 and following the death of the owner and a period in store at the NRM, No 69023 was purchased by the NELPG in 1982; still owned by the group, the locomotive is based on the Wensleydale Railway although at the time of writing is out of service undergoing a major overhaul with a planned return to service date of 2024. *Phil Tatt/Online Transport Archive*

Looking resplendent in its newly-applied maroon livery, Ivatt 2-6-2T No 41241 is pictured standing in front of the goods shed at Haworth on 3 June 1968; less than a month later the locomotive was in use hauling the line's reopening special. *Alexander McBlain/Online Transport Archive*

It is 29 June 1968 and amidst the crowds at Keighley station the reopening special hauled by Nos 41241 and 72 awaits departure. The actual reopening ceremony was carried out by the Mayor of Keighley, Alderman James Henry Waterworth, who cut a ribbon in front of the train. The Mayor was accompanied by his wife and by Bob Cryer, the chairman of the preservation society and later the MP for Keighley. *Gavin Morrison*

The reopening special arrives at Oxenhope on 29 June 1968 to be greeted by a significant crowd on the platform. With the reopening of the line after six years, the rust that is evident on the railheads could be consigned to history. *Gavin Morrison*

Seen shortly after the line's reopening in June 1968, Ivatt 2-6-2T No 41241 is seen running round its train at Oxenhope in the non-standard maroon and black livery that it was repainted in prior to the line's reopening. The popularity of the line was evinced by the 35,000 tickets sold in the first six months of operation as a preserved line. *Michael H. Waller/Author's collection*

CONSOLIDATION

With the line successfully reopened, it was to prove an immediate success with some 2,000 passengers being carried per week by September. That month was to witness another 'first' in preservation when ex-MR Class 4F No 43924 arrived from the famous Woodham Bros scrapyard in Barry, South Wales. This was the first of some 200 steam locomotives to be acquired from the scrapyard for preservation; previously there had been restrictions on the resale of ex-BR locomotives sold for scrap but the lifting of these permitted the preservation movement to secure most of the steam locomotives sold to Dai Woodham in the mid-1960s. Unlike many of the locomotives salvaged from the yard in later years, No 43924 was still in a condition that enabled it to be moved by rail; over a period of two days during September 1968 it was towed north by four diesels in total – Nos D1699, D338, D373 and D6946 – and, on arrival at Keighley, was towed to Haworth behind ex-MSC No 31. Over the next two years,

On 27 October 1968, the ex-North Western Gas Board Peckett 0-4-0T, new originally in 1941, stands with a one-coach train at Haworth with plenty of passengers on the platform. Too small for the line, the locomotive left the railway on loan in 1974 but remained the KWVR's property until it was acquired by the Ribble Steam Railway following its transfer there in 1999. *Gavin Morrison*

Manchester Ship Canal 0-6-0T No 67 is seen on a Boxing Day afternoon service ready to leave Oxenhope for Haworth in 1969. Note the use of the old gentleman's coach associated with *The Railway Children*. No 67 is an example of the MSC's 'long tank' of Hudswell Clarke supplied locomotives; this was because of its 850 gallon tank capacity as opposed to the 580 gallon capacity of the 'short tank' design, such as No 31 *Hamburg*. The MSC network was one of the largest non-nationalised railway networks in Britain and No 67 was supplied by Hudswell Clarke & Co Ltd in 1919 (Works No 1369). Rendered redundant in the 1960s as a result of the dieselisation and rationalisation of the MSC network, No 67 was secured for preservation in 1969 and so was a relatively recent arrival on the line when recorded here. Since leaving the KWVR, No 67 has been based on a number of lines but, since 2012 when it was donated to the line, it has been based on the Middleton Railway in Leeds, close to where it was constructed more than a century ago. *Gavin Morrison*

No 43924 was restored and when returned to service in 1970 was to be the first ex-Barry locomotive to be restored to an operational condition.

Another arrival was Stanier 'Black 5' No 45212. One of the type to be built by Armstrong Whitworth – in 1935 – as LMS No 5212, the locomotive had originally been based in Bradford. Achieving fame as providing the motive power for BR's last standard gauge main-line revenue-earning service on 4 August 1968, the locomotive – by now allocated to Lostock Hall shed in Preston – was acquired by the KWVR in full working order from BR and arrived on the branch in October 1968. A more powerful

One of the most bizarre liveries to appear in the preservation era must have been the wallpapering of Class 5 No 5212 on the KWVR to demonstrate how good a type of glue was at sticking things. The locomotive in its unusual finish is seen on 4 February 1969 at Haworth with a service bound for Oxenhope. *Gavin Morrison*

Steam in the snow. On 9 February 1969, during the line's first operational winter as a preserved railway, Class J72 0-6-0T No 69023 *Joem* awaits departure from Haworth with a service to Oxenhope. *John Meredith/Online Transport Archive*

locomotive – capable of taking six carriages over the steeply-graded branch unaided – the 'Black 5' was pressed into service immediately to cater for the heavier trains that the railway anticipated as passenger traffic increased. In early 1969 – and prior to being repainted into black livery – No 45212 was to cause some consternation as it was covered in red and cream wallpaper for use in the filming of a television advert for Solvite. This was not to be the locomotive's only experience of filming during 1969; on 16 June it was used – surrounded by sheep – for the production of the Yorkshire Television serial *Tom Grattan's War*. The next day saw the ex-LYR 0-6-0 'Ironclad' No 957 – by now fully restored – used in service for the first time since its withdrawal a decade earlier during the shooting of the film *The Private Life of Sherlock Holmes*.

Another tender locomotive to reach the KWVR was Hughes-designed 2-6-0 No 42700. This was the pioneer of the type and was built originally at Horwich in 1926 as No 13000. Withdrawn in March 1966 from Birkenhead shed, the locomotive was acquired by the

The 'Black Five' was not to retain its unusual livery for long; on 30 March 1969 it is again pictured at Haworth, this time with an Up service towards Keighley. Completed at Armstrong Whitworth in November 1935, No 45212 spent its final twenty years of service allocated to sheds in north-west England; its final reallocation – in January 1968 – saw it move to Lostock Hall and was to survive through until almost the very end of main-line steam operation on BR, being taken out of service after operating the last regular steam-hauled passenger train on BR on 4 August 1968. Preserved on withdrawal, No 45212 was moved to the KWVR in October 1968. Based on the line until 2000, when it was transferred to the North Yorkshire Moors Railway, No 45212 returned to the KWVR in 2011 towards the end of its then current boiler certificate. The locomotive was fully overhauled at Bury between 2013 and 2016; this work also included equipping No 45212 for main-line operation and since then the locomotive, although based on the KWVR, has seen service on steam specials in Scotland – on the West Highland line – and elsewhere. *John Worley/Online Transport Archive*

The Leeds-based Hudswell Clarke & Co Ltd supplied a large number of steam locomotives to the privately-owned railway that once served the Manchester Ship Canal. Completed in 1903 (Works No 679) was No 31 (originally named *Hamburg*), seen here in the yard at Haworth in the spring of 1969. However, due to the inevitable anti-German feeling engendered during the First World War and following pressure from the dock workers, its name was dropped; it was only restored, after preservation, in March 1972. Withdrawn in the mid-1960s as the MSC's railway network was dieselised and rationalised, No 31 arrived on the railway in June 1967. Modified to permit its use on passenger services, the locomotive was, however, restricted in its use as a result of the line's gradients. No 31 has been out of use for a number of years and is now displayed at Oxenhope. *Phil Tatt/Online Transport Archive*

National Collection. However, with the collection lacking the space to accommodate all its exhibits, a number were loaned out and No 42700 moved to Haworth in the middle of 1968. Restored to LMS livery as No 2700 by the end of that year, permission was granted for the KWVR to use the 'Crab' on occasional services, and it was introduced back to operation during 1969.

More locomotives and items of rolling stock were also appearing. On 18 January 1969, an ex-NCB 'Austerity' 0-6-0ST *'Fred'* arrived; it had been delayed in transit as a result of hot boxes and thus had to be worked on before it could enter service. Coaching stock acquired in early 1969 included an ex-MR six-wheel luggage composite and two BR Standard Mark 1 suburban coaches, both of which were acquired from operational service; these were non-corridor second class No 46228 (which was to be eventually scrapped in 1984) and open second with lavatory No 48007 (which was scrapped in 1976). During

No 957 was one of two locomotives that were painted in a fictitious livery for the filming of *The Railway Children*; the other was ex-LT 0-6-0PT No L89, which is pictured sporting this livery alongside the shed at Haworth in early 1970. Although out of service, the locomotive was cosmetically restored to the livery it carried here for display at the NRM and at the museum's Shildon out-station in May 2014. It returned to the railway in 2017 and remains on static display at Oxenhope. The locomotive requires major investment if it is to return to steam and so is likely to remain a static exhibit for the foreseeable future. *Harry Luff/Online Transport Archive*

In June 1969, 'USA' tank No 72 approaches Haworth station with a service towards Keighley as a good crowd of passengers wait on the platform for its arrival. No 72 was one of fourteen locomotives acquired by the Southern Railway after the Second World War from the USATC for use primarily on shunting work at Southampton Docks; a fifteenth was also acquired but only as a source of spare parts and never used in service. No 72 – later BR No 30072 – was built originally by Vulcan Iron Works of Wilkes-Barre in Pennsylvania in 1943. Allocated variously to Willesden, Cricklewood and Guildford sheds, as well as Southampton, No 30072 was withdrawn in July 1967 and acquired for preservation from the scrap line at Salisbury the following month. With an enlarged coal bunker, the locomotive was the most heavily used on the line until 1973. Equipped for oil firing in 1976, it was to revert to coal burning in 1987. By this date the locomotive was not powerful enough to handle the heavier trains that the Worth Valley was operating and also required a major – and expensive – overhaul. As a result, it has spent much of the last three decades on static display before being transferred, following a change of ownership in 2015, to the Ribble Steam Railway. *John Worley/Online Transport Archive*

the summer of the year a second 'Black 5' – No 5025 owned by W.E.C. Watkinson of the Scottish Railway Preservation Society – was based on the railway; it was used during July on a number of services as it was run-in following overhaul by the Hunslet Engine Co Ltd of Leeds. This was followed by an 0-6-0ST '*Isabel*' that arrived in August; this was built by Hawthorn Leslie in 1919 and acquired from ICI at Blakeley, near Manchester. On 31 August, the eighteenth locomotive to have been steamed on the railway since its preservation was ex-LMS No 11243; this was the second of the ex-LYR 0-4-0ST 'Pugs' based on the line and had been undergoing restoration at Haworth. Sister locomotive No 51218 returned to the railway, after a thirty-month break, in October 1969.

Mid-1969 saw the railway achieve its first – and successful – year of operation. The railway's first Easter service – from 3 to 7 April 1969 – resulted in no fewer than 4,500 passengers travelling, of whom more than a third travelled on Easter Monday. Fundraising was in progress to build a shed at Oxenhope with some £450 raised of the £2,500 required; towards the end of the year more than £600 had been subscribed to the project. Work on the construction of the 120ft x 30ft shed was undertaken in early 1970 and by the spring was in use as a paint shop; amongst the first locomotives to receive attention there were the two 'Black 5s' – No 5025 was restored to LMS livery but No 45212 appeared in BR black but with a KWVLR crest on its tender.

In many ways, 1970 was the year that saw the line achieve national – if not international – fame as the classic children's film *The Railway Children* starring Bernard Cribbins, who sadly passed away whilst this book was being written, and Jenny Agutter was shot on the line. The shooting of the much-loved film involved a number of locomotives – the Gresley 'N2' 0-6-2T, LYR 0-6-0 No 957 (which was repainted into a green livery with 'GN & SR' – for Great Northern & Southern Railway – on its tender sides), ex-MSC 0-6-0T No 67 and ex-GWR/LT No L89 (which was repainted into a predominantly brown livery with 'GN & SR' emblazoned on its tanks) – in the dramatisation of E.E. Nesbitt's story.

On the same day, No 72 is seen again, this time emerging from the 75yd-long Mytholmes Tunnel with a service towards Oxenhope. The tunnel was opened on 6 November 1892 following powers obtained the previous year to construct a slight deviation off the original route. *John Worley/Online Transport Archive*

Built by Armstrong Whitworth in Newcastle during November 1935, No 45212 was based at Low Moor shed prior to nationalisation and saw service on LMS services from Bradford or Leeds across the Pennines on the former LYR route via Halifax. Although it therefore had a local connection, its post-nationalisation career saw it exclusively allocated west of the Pennines, being withdrawn from Lostock Hall in August 1968. It is pictured here in the yard at Haworth in June 1969. *John Worley/Online Transport Archive*

The success of the film was reflected in a significant growth in the railway's passenger traffic; this was already growing nicely – the total number carried in 1970 was, at some 70,000, an increase of about 10,000 over the number carried in the previous year – but it was reported in the summer of 1971 that passenger traffic had more than doubled in the period up to 18 April, from 10,140 in 1970 to 20,889 in 1971. One of the factors in the increase in passenger traffic in 1970 was the introduction of the first Father Christmas Specials; these operated on two days – the last two Sundays before Christmas Day (the 13th and the 20th) – and a total of 2,543 were carried over the two days. A total of twelve locomotives were used in service during 1970; the highest mileage being achieved by the 'USA' 0-6-0T No 72, with a total of 1,735. At the other extreme, the Class J72 0-6-0T 69023 *Joem* achieved thirty.

Work at Keighley to extend the platform and station-limit working now permitted the operation of seven-coach trains – with a capacity of 575 passengers – with the aim of ensuring that 95 per cent of passengers had a seat. Another significant development was the construction of the loop at Damems; work on the construction of this commenced in early March 1971 with the new facility being commissioned on 30 May 1971. The new loop, with a capacity to handle a locomotive plus six carriages, permitted the operation of a two-train service. One of the restrictions on the operation of large locomotives

Recorded at Oxenhope on 3 November 1968 is an impressive line up of vintage rolling stock. The coaches are, from the left, Nos E900270E, DE953003, Sc45038M and E900269E. A fuller history of Nos DE953003 and E900269E can be found on pages 29 and 68 respectively. No E900270E was originally an NER open first four-wheel carriage No 1173 constructed at York in 1869. Converted into an Officer's Saloon during the 1890s and repaired in the early 1920s, the coach remained in use until 1967 when it was purchased privately for preservation. Following its stay on the Worth Valley, it moved initially to the Derwent Valley line, near York, before being stored near Northallerton. Based on the Tanfield Railway since 1993, its restoration was completed in 1997. No Sc45038M had been built for the LYR at Newton Heath as six-wheel Directors' Saloon No 1 in 1878. Rebuilt as a bogie coach in 1908, it remained in use until the early 1960s – by now allocated to Inverness on the Scottish Region well away from its home area. Preserved in 1965 and still based on the KWVR, the coach is now displayed at Oxenhope where its exterior has been fully restored and work proceeds on the completion of its interior. *John Meredith/Online Transport Archive*

or double-heading on the line was the length of the headshunt at Oxenhope; another project completed during the spring of 1971 was the extension of the headshunt. Later in the year, the railway accommodated an out-of-gauge load when the redundant ex-MR box from Frizinghall, on the Shipley to Bradford Forster Square line, was moved on 14 November by rail from Oakworth to the loop. Fully restored and commissioned on 5 May 1973, the box still controls the loop. The opening of the box meant that the line could either be operated on the basis of one locomotive in steam or by two tokens – Oxenhope to Damems and Damems to Keighley.

Alongside the development of the railway, the line's collection of locomotives continued to grow. In December 1970, ex-Taff Vale Railway Class O2 0-6-2T No 85 arrived. This locomotive, which had been built in 1899 by the Glasgow-based Neilson Reid, had been withdrawn by the GWR in 1927 and sold two years later to the Lambton, Hetton

Pictured in the yard at Haworth on 8 June 1969 is an Andrew Barclay-built 0-4-0T (Works No 2226). Built in 1946 for use by ICI at the company's Dyestuffs Division Works at Huddersfield, the locomotive was rendered redundant following dieselisation in 1967. Presented to the KWVR, the locomotive arrived at Haworth in April 1968. Of limited use to the railway due to its short wheelbase, the locomotive was used intermittently until its boiler certificate expired. It was then placed on display at Oxenhope until it was sold; moved to Cheshire in 1992, the locomotive was displayed in a garden centre until the middle of the last decade when it was purchased by a volunteer on the Churnet Valley Railway and relocated to Cheddleton. At the time of writing, work on its restoration had yet to commence. *John Worley/Online Transport Archive*

& Joicey Colliery Co in County Durham. Passing to the NCB at nationalisation in 1947, No 52 – as it had become – was finally to be withdrawn in 1968. When preservation was first mooted, it was thought that the locomotive might go to the North Norfolk Railway, but it was offered to – and accepted by – the KWVR. During the summer, following the failure of the plan to preserve part (or all) of the Longmoor Military Railway, one of that line's 'Austerity' 0-6-0Ts – WD118 *Brussels* (built by Hudswell Clarke: Works No 1782 of 1945) – arrived at Haworth. This locomotive was unusual in that it was oil – rather than coal – fired. On 22 August 1971, BR Standard 2-6-4T No 80002 was introduced to service following its restoration.

Late 1971 saw the acquisition of a further two locomotives from Barry. 'West Country' No 34092 *City of Wells* was delivered by road to Ingrow on 27 October 1971; it was then towed up the line to Haworth by the newly-restored No 80002 on 7 November 1971. The Standard tank was driven by the designer of the Standard classes, Robert A. Riddles, who had been guest of honour at the railway's annual dinner the previous evening. This was followed by the arrival of Stanier-designed Class 8F 2-8-0 No 48431 on 3 June 1972.

Initially regarded as a long-term restoration project, No 48431 was actually returned to service in December 1975. The number of operational locomotives on the line was further increased during the summer of 1972, with the restoration of the ex-LYR 0-6-0ST No 752 that steamed for the first time for more than a decade on 22 July. The locomotive, designed by William Barton Wright and built by Beyer, Peacock & Co in May 1881, was withdrawn in 1937 and sold into industrial use. Preserved in 1966 and initially stored at Heap Bridge, it had been transferred to Haworth in October 1971. A further locomotive rescued from Barry – BR Standard Class 4 4-6-0 No 75078 – arrived on 24 June 1972; initially restoration work was undertaken at Oakworth but the locomotive was transferred to Haworth in late 1972 and the locomotive re-entered service in February 1977. Following experimental use of the oil-fired *Brussels*, the railway decided to convert 'USA' tank No 72 to oil firing.

Also pictured in the yard at Haworth on 8 June 1969 is the ex-Darwen Gas Works 0-4-0ST. Built by Peckett & Co in 1941 (Works No 1999), the locomotive was constructed for the Crowlands Gas Works at Southport. It was transferred to Darwen in 1958 and survived in use until it was replaced by a diesel five years later. Sold, following the intervention of the KWVR's then chairman Bob Cryer, to the KWVR, it arrived at Haworth after three years of storage in September 1966. Following the fitting of air brakes, the locomotive was used for some years on passenger services, but it was unsuitable for heavier trains and in September 1974 it was transferred on long-term loan to the Steamport Museum at Southport (appropriately). Seeing service at Steamport, following the closure of the museum in 1999, it was transferred to the Ribble Steam Railway. With ownership now held by the Ribble Steam Railway, work on restoring the locomotive is in hand at the time of writing. *John Worley/Online Transport Archive*

Pictured in the yard at Haworth on 8 June 1969 is Manning Wardle (Works No 1210) 0-6-0T *Sir Berkeley*. New in 1890, the locomotive was initially owned by the contractors Logan & Hemingway and used on a number of engineering projects; these included the London extension of the Manchester, Sheffield & Lincolnshire Railway. When Logan & Hemingway went into liquidation in 1935, the locomotive was acquired by the Kettering-based Cranford Ironstone Co; it was under its new ownership that the locomotive gained its name. Modified in the early 1950s, *Sir Berkeley* was rendered largely redundant later in the decade when the company acquired a new locomotive to replace it. Transferred in 1959 to the quarries at Byfield, it was withdrawn the following year and stored. Rescued for preservation in 1964, the locomotive was moved to the KWVR and was reunited with its original weatherboard – discovered more than a decade after it was removed and replaced at Cranford – as illustrated here. Owned by the VCT for some 50 years, following its purchase in the mid-1970s, the locomotive was fitted with a replacement boiler in 2006 (its boiler certificate having expired in 2001). The locomotive re-entered service on the Middleton Railway – where it is currently based – on 14 April 2007. With its most recent boiler certificate again having expired, *Sir Berkeley* is at the time of writing out of service pending an overhaul. *John Worley/Online Transport Archive*

There were two significant additions to the locomotive fleet during 1973. The first of these was one of the wartime 'Austerity' 2-8-0s designed by Riddles. Constructed by Vulcan Foundry in January 1945, the locomotive was sold when virtually brand-new to Nederlandse Spoorwegen, becoming No 4484, but was destined to have only a short life in The Netherlands before it was sold to Statens Järnvägar – the Swedish state railways – in 1953. Withdrawn in October 1956, as No 1931, the locomotive was then allocated to Sweden's strategic reserve before being finally sold for preservation in late 1972. It arrived by boat at Hull on 12 January 1973 and was delivered by road to Ingrow on the following day. The second major arrival of 1973 was the last steam locomotive constructed for BR: Class 9F 2-10-0 No 92220 *Evening Star*. The locomotive, part of the National Collection, was transferred to the Worth Valley on loan and arrived during the summer after being on display at Tyseley over the weekend of 2/3 June.

No 92220's new home was to be the extended green shed at Oxenhope; work on the extension of the existing structure started in early 1973 and was completed by the spring. When finished, the building comprised three tracks some 240ft in length. The completed structure was formally opened by the Mayor of Keighley on 14 April 1973; this was appropriate as part of the work had been funded by a loan by Keighley Borough Council – a body that was to disappear with local government reform on 1 April 1974 – which was subsequently repaid. It was the aim that, with this structure and the other sheds on the line, delivered all the line's locomotives could be stored in undercover accommodation. The agreement seeing No 92220 on loan permitted its use on the line, making it by far the largest steam locomotive ever to have operated the branch. With the completion of the extended green shed, work commenced on the extension of the older shed at Oxenhope in order to convert it into a carriage works.

The early 1970s witnessed an almost inexorable increase in passenger traffic; partly this was the result of the ongoing impact of the publicity generated by the line's regular

On 7 July 1969, No 41241 is seen approaching Haworth station bunker-first with a service towards Keighley. Built at Crewe Works during September 1949, the locomotive was allocated to Skipton shed from August 1965 where, paradoxically, it was allocated the Worth Valley branch duty – despite the line having been closed completely earlier in the decade. The locomotive was noted regularly having made the trip to Keighley light engine from Skipton; it then spent several hours idling before returning to its shed later in the afternoon. Withdrawn in December 1966, it made one final trip – under its own steam – to Keighley. Now based on the railway for more than 50 years, No 41241 was returned to operational condition in 2018. *John Worley/Online Transport Archive*

In May and June 1969, the KWVR took delivery of three of the redundant RSH-built 0-6-0STs, nicknamed 'Uglies', that had been constructed for use by the Northamptonshire iron and steel manufacturers Stewarts & Lloyds. There was an extensive network of mineral lines that served the county's ironstone pits, providing a link through to the major steelworks at Corby. One of these pits – at Harringworth – was only linked to the main network after the Second World War and Stewarts & Lloyds acquired seven locomotives – Nos 56-62 – in 1950; these were supplemented by a further two – Nos 63 and 64 – four years later. Following dieselisation in 1969, all nine were withdrawn with Nos 57, 62 and 63 being preserved on the KWVR. Here No 63 is pictured awaiting departure from Keighley during the autumn of 1969. All three saw service on the line for a period but have subsequently departed. No 62 was the first to go in 1982; this locomotive is now based on the Spa Valley Railway, having received the boiler from No 57 in order to restore it to an operational condition. Its most recent boiler certificate expired in January 2021. No 57 departed from the KWVR in the 1990s; having donated its original boiler to assist with the restoration of No 62, No 57 is now on static display at the Spa Valley Railway. The last of the trio to depart was No 63, again in the 1990s; this locomotive was operational most recently on the Great Central Railway but again its most recent boiler certificate, following its return to steam in December 2011, has expired. *Harry Luff/Online Transport Archive*

appearances on film and television but also by the increased capacity offered by the loop at Damems. In 1972, a total of 125,629 tickets were sold – an increase of 77 per cent over 1971 – whilst in 1973 the figure increased by a further 6 per cent to a total of 133,040. Another consequence of the increased capacity was an increase in the mileage operated; this increased 9 per cent between 1972 and 1973. There was a slight blip, however, in 1974 when passenger traffic declined by 3 per cent but this was more than offset by a reduction in more than 9 per cent in the mileage operated.

As the railway matured so it looked at increasing revenue through special events. Mention has already been made of the introduction of what subsequently became the hugely successful Santa Specials but in 1973 the railway held its first Enthusiasts' Day when a more intensive service was operated. This event was repeated in 1974 when more than 2,000 tickets were sold and a wide range of locomotives – including No 92220 and 'Black 5' No 45212 – were operated. Linked to this event, on 30 March 1974, the railway got involved with its first charter train, with a three-car DMU bringing passengers from Lancashire via Hellifield to Keighley. The following year – when the event was held on 22 March – there were no fewer than six locomotives in steam; these included ex-LYR 0-6-0 No 957 which had been repainted to its BR livery as No 52044. From these relatively small beginnings, the various galas – which are such of a feature of this and other preserved lines – have developed over the years.

When the railway was first established, it took a lease on only platform 4 at Keighley station; in late 1975 the railway took on the lease of a second platform – No 3 – which again allowed for greater flexibility of operation and increased capacity. Following track alteration work, the new facility came into use; it proved its worth over the weekend of 3 and 4 April 1976 when, catering for more than 4,000 passengers, six locomotives were in use during the Enthusiasts' Weekend. A fortnight later, over the Easter weekend, a further 12,000 travelled over the line. This was the most successful Easter since the line's reopening.

The railway's range of motive power was increased by the entry into service of Class 8F No 8431 following its restoration from ex-Barry condition. The locomotive had hauled its

The yard at Oxenhope in October 1969 with some of the railway's historic coaching stock stabled. With the development of the facilities at Oxenhope, this view has radically altered over the past fifty years. Initially it was planned that the railway's locomotive stock would be based at Oxenhope and the goods shed was extended to provide facilities but, with the continued use of Haworth, the carriage and wagon department made use of the enlarged building. In 2000, following the receipt of a £600,000 grant from the Heritage Lottery Fund, a two-road carriage shed, capable of accommodating twenty-four coaches, was completed for the stock used on service trains. *Michael H. Waller/Author's Collection*

On a bleak 31 January 1970, one of the line's two Waggon und Maschinenbau railbuses – No M79964 in its Worth Valley livery – is pictured arriving into Keighley station. This and companion No 79962 were part of a batch of five railbuses supplied by the German manufacturer to BR in April 1958; based originally on the Eastern Region where they saw service on the branches to Braintree, Maldon and Saffron Waldon, the quintet was designed – along with the other railbuses delivered – to reduce operational costs on loss-making lines. Whilst this was achieved, the lines continued to be loss making and so were mostly closed. Three of the Waggon und Maschinenbau railbuses – including No 79964 – had their original Büssing 150hp engines replaced by similar units produced by AEC as a result of the costs of obtaining spares from Germany. Two – again including No 79964 – were tested on the Alston branch, but proved unsuitable, before ending their lives in Derbyshire. All five were withdrawn between November 1964 and April 1967; apart from the two preserved on the KWVR, two others of the batch also survive and are currently based on the Ribble Steam Railway (No 79960) and at the East Anglia Railway Museum (No 79963). *Geoffrey Tribe/Online Transport Archive*

first service on 6 December 1975 when, in conjunction with the Swedish 2-8-0 No 1931, it had been used to haul a train in connection with a party that had arrived on the line via the Settle & Carlisle line on a special organised by the Wirral Railway Circle. A further special service was operated on 15 May 1976 when passengers on a charter organised by the Erlestoke Manor Fund had a return trip to Oxenhope behind Class 4F No 43924 prior to heading north over the Settle & Carlisle line.

Across the pond, the USA celebrated its bicentenary in 1976 and, to mark the event, the railway renumbered 'USA' 0-6-0T No 72, which had just been repainted in its brown livery but adorned with the Stars & Stripes, 1776. Another repaint saw one of the two railbuses – No E79962 – restored to its original BR green livery; at the same time sister No E79964 appeared in a Deutsche Bundesbahn-inspired red livery.

The following year – the Queen's Silver Jubilee – saw an exchange in terms of the locomotives on loan to the railway from the NRM when, on 20 May 1977, Class 9F No 92220 *Evening Star* brought ex-GNR 4-4-2 No 990 *Henry Oakley* to the railway and returned to York hauling the ex-LMS 2-6-0 No 2700. In 1978 No 92220 was to make a further brief visit to the line when on 2 September 1978, it visited the branch in connection with the railway's memorial service for Bishop Eric Treacy, the president of the preservation society, who had died earlier in the year. The GNR Atlantic was not to be the only addition to the line's locomotive stock during 1977; later in the year it was announced that the purchase of a USATC Class S160 2-8-0, built by the American Locomotive Co of Schenectady, New York in 1945, from Poland had been agreed. Polish State Railways No 474 was shipped from Gdynia to Hull in October and was first test steamed at Haworth on 26 November 1977 prior to undergoing an overhaul with a view to entering service during 1978.

Towards the end of the year a significant event occurred when, on 8 October 1977, the line welcomed its first through train. This was a special organised by the SRPS from Falkirk. Using seven of the SRPS's own coaches and hauled by Class 25 No 25068 through from Scotland to Keighley, the special was double-headed from Keighley to Oxenhope and return by No 990 and BR Standard 4-6-0 No 75078. The following year – on 30 September 1978 – the first through train using BR coaching stock operated over the line when eight carriages formed a special operated by the Roch Valley Railway Society from Castleton, Rochdale and Oldham. The special was double-headed to Oxenhope by '8F' No 8431 and 'USA' tank No 72. A week later, on 7 October, the SRPS repeated its special when eight coaches headed south from Falkirk.

The year 1978 marked the tenth anniversary of the line's reopening and a number of events or activities were organised to mark the date. One feature was a special postmark

Recorded the same day is Platform 4 at Keighley station; at this date, the KWVR only operated into this platform and the adjacent Platform 3 is out of use and in poor condition; it was only in late 1975 that agreement was reached for the railway to lease Platform 3 as well. This acquisition allowed locomotives off KWVR trains to run round in Keighley station rather than having to propel the trains out of the station prior to running round. *Geoffrey Tribe/Online Transport Archive*

Later on the same day, No 79964 stands in the platform at Oxenhope station. *Geoffrey Tribe/Online Transport Archive*

The station forecourt at Oxenhope on 31 January 1970 before the work started on the gradual expansion of the facilities at the station and the improvements to the car park. *Geoffrey Tribe/Online Transport Archive*

In the mid-1950s, with modernisation of the railway network on the agenda, it was clear that diesel and electric traction represented the future for the industry. As a result, a number of experimental and prototype locomotives were constructed; these included the Vulcan Foundry-built No D0226 (No D226 until it was renumbered in August 1959 following the delivery of English Electric Type 4 – later Class 40 – No D226), which was one of a number of locomotives constructed by English Electric in the period. The locomotive, which had electric transmission (unlike sister No D0227 which was a diesel-hydraulic), was completed in 1957 and spent three years in service with BR. The two locomotives did not prove to be a great success as they were unsuitable for shunting duties but experience with them demonstrated – as far as English Electric was concerned – the superiority of electric over hydraulic transmission. Returned to its manufacturer in 1960 (having last been allocated to Bristol St Philip's Marsh), the locomotive was placed on permanent loan to the KWVR in 1966. On the preserved railway it has found its niche, being powerful enough to haul both works trains and passenger services. It is seen here in the yard at Haworth during the autumn of 1970. *Peter Watson Collection/Online Transport Archive*

featuring No 51218 that was used on all mail franked in Keighley as well as first class mail from Bradford; this was in use over the summer until 29 September. Although the actual anniversary of the reopening was on 29 June, due to shooting of the film *Yanks* on the line – an event that required two of the line's 2-8-0s ('8F' No 8431 and USATC No 5820) to head light engine to Shipley for turning on the triangle there – a special train was run with invited guests, including three children born on 29 June 1968, on 22 June 1978; one of the two pioneering locomotives – No 72 – was used to haul the special as the other – No 41241 – was out of service at the time. One of the consequences of the

The KWVR was the first preserved railway to operate Santa Specials. Pictured is one of the first to operate, on 13 December 1970, seen at Oxenhope headed by the two locomotives — 'USA' 0-6-0T No 72 and Ivatt 2-6-2T No 41241 — that had operated the opening special two years earlier in their non-standard liveries. The crowd demonstrates the success of the venture and why other railways soon followed the KWVR's lead. *Gavin Morrison*

Late BR or early preservation? On a dank day – 31 January 1971 – 0-6-0ST No 67 is shrouded in steam as it prepares to depart from Oxenhope with a three-coach train. The ambience of the station – even down to the slightly ropy condition of the platform and the lack of passengers – could have epitomised the railway in the final days of its operation by BR. There is a paradox in railway preservation: the more successful the line – and the Worth Valley has undoubtedly been very successful – the greater the risk that the line's unique character can be lost. *John Meredith/Online Transport Archive*

Spreading the word; marketing of a preserved railway takes many forms. On 30 August 1971, 0-6-0T *Sir Berkeley* was displayed on a low loader at Harewood House on the occasion of a traction engine rally in the house's grounds. *John Meredith/Online Transport Archive*

Pictured in Ingrow yard on 30 October 1971, shortly after its arrival from the famous Woodham Bros scrapyard at Barry, is unrebuilt 'West Country' No 34092 *City of Wells*. Completed at Brighton Works in September 1949, No 34092 was initially allocated to service on the Southern's main lines to Kent. Following the electrification of these routes, No 34092 was reallocated to Salisbury in May 1961, from where it was withdrawn in November 1964. One of the large number of locomotives sold to Woodham Bros, it reached Barry in March 1965. Purchased for preservation six years later, the locomotive's poor external condition is all too evident in this view as Standard 2-6-4T No 80002 heads towards Oxenhope with a service train. Restoration of No 34092 to operational condition would take nearly a decade. *Gavin Morrison*

In October 1960, to mark the final closure of its tramway system, Sheffield Corporation decorated two trams with scenes of the city's tramway history. No 510 was acquired by the Tramway Museum Society and is now based at the National Tramway Museum at Crich; the other – No 513 – has, however, had a much more nomadic existence. Stored for a period on the Middleton Railway, where it was fortunate to avoid the damage wrought by vandals on other preserved trams based there, No 513 spent some time stored in the ex-GNR goods shed at Cullingworth. Briefly the tram was based at Oxenhope and is pictured in the yard there during the autumn of 1971. Subsequently, No 513 was to be based at Embsay and at Beamish; since 2011 it has been at the East Anglia Transport Museum at Carlton Colville. Although fully restored, it has lost its decorative panels. *Peter Watkins Collection/Online Transport Archive*

contract to film *Yanks* was that total ticket sales in 1978 at almost 147,000 were slightly lower than the previous year as filming coincided with a period when school specials would normally have run. Earlier in the year the railway announced a further major development: it was to seek planning permission for the construction of a major new shed at Haworth to supplement the existing workshop in the erstwhile goods shed.

In conjunction with the Post Office, the railway launched a railway letter service on 9 May 1979; the first letter was despatched from Haworth by Councillor A. Hodgson, who was the then Assistant Lord Mayor of Bradford. The issuing of special railway stamps – such as the quartet issued in April 1981 to help fund work at Wakefield Cathedral (where

Amongst the first locomotives to receive attention in the new shed at Oxenhope following its completion in early 1970 was 'Black 5' No 5025, which was restored to its LMS livery. The locomotive is seen here, after repainting, at Keighley during the early autumn of 1970. New in 1934, the 'Black 5' was one of the class to survive through until the end of main-line steam on BR, being withdrawn following use on part of the LCGB 'Farewell to Steam' special on 4 August 1968 when it and sister No 45390 took the train from Carnforth via Hellifield and Blackburn to Lostock Hall Junction. Having spent the first year of its life based in Scotland, it was selected by the late Ted Watkinson for preservation and possible use on the proposed Strathspey Railway. Overhauled by the Hunslet Locomotive Co in Leeds during 1969, it was based on the KWVR between then and 1974 when it headed northwards. Again overhauled, this time by Andrew Barclay of Kilmarnock, it entered service on the Strathspey in August 1975. Withdrawn in 1993, the locomotive was restored to service in May 2021. *Peter Watson Collection/Online Transport Archive*

the railway's late president, the Right Reverend Eric Treacy, had been Bishop) – have been a feature of fundraising activities over the years.

August 1979 witnessed another arrival on the line in the guise of 'Jinty' 0-6-0T No 47279 from Woodham Bros scrapyard. The locomotive had originally been withdrawn from Sutton Oak, St Helens, shed in December 1966 and had been sold for scrap the following year. Having spent more than a decade rusting in South Wales, the restoration of the locomotive was a major project, not being completed until February 1988. Whilst one ex-Barry locomotive arrived on the line, the restoration of another – unrebuilt 'West Country' No 34092 *City of Wells* – was completed after eight years. The locomotive officially re-entered service in April 1980.

Above: **The last** of the original batch of RSH-built 0-6-0STs supplied to Stewarts & Lloyds in 1950 was No 62 which is seen here in the yard at Haworth in the early autumn of 1971. This was the first of the trio to depart the Worth Valley; it was sold, after awaiting a boiler repair for a number of years, and moved to the East Lancashire Railway. Seeing service thereafter on a number of preserved lines – including the North Yorkshire Moors Railway, the Lavender Line and the Bodmin & Wenford – the locomotive was acquired in 2007 by a member of the Spa Valley Railway in Kent. Work started in January 2008 on its overhaul; this was completed using parts, including the boiler, from sister locomotive No 57 in October 2010. The locomotive's most recent boiler certificate expired in January 2021, and it awaits a further overhaul at the time of writing. *Peter Watson Collection/Online Transport Archive*

Opposite above: **Two of** the line's then collection of pre-Grouping carriages are pictured at Oxenhope on 1 July 1972. On the left is six-wheel saloon No 900269E. This had originally been built at York in 1891 by the North Eastern Railway as officers' saloon No 41 and had subsequently been LNER No 241. This remained on the line until the mid-1970s when it moved to Embsay. Subsequently housed in Derbyshire and on the Tanfield Railway, it was acquired by the Aln Valley Railway about a decade ago and is now based at the railway's Alnwick station, where it is undergoing restoration, On the right is ex-Manchester, Sheffield & Lincolnshire Railway; whilst its MSLR number is unknown, it subsequently became Great Central No 176. This had been built at Dukinfield in 1876; becoming LNER No 5176 at Grouping, it was latterly numbered DE953003 in the BR departmental stock. Part of the Vintage Carriage Trust collection, a two-year restoration programme was completed in 1985. *John Meredith/Online Transport Archive*

Opposite below: **On 10 December** 1972, BR Standard 2-6-4T No 80002 and Class 5 No 5025 are pictured departing from the yard at Haworth with empty stock prior to operating passenger services that day. *Charles Firminger/Bob Bridger Collection/Online Transport Archive*

Above: **Later the** same day, the two locomotives are seen heading from Keighley with the 12.25pm service to Oxenhope. The background of the view is dominated by the large goods shed that was built for the GNR. Freight facilities were withdrawn from the yard – which was known as Keighley South from March 1951 – on 17 July 1961. More than sixty years after closure, however, the substantial stone built shed remains and is in commercial use as a builders' merchants. *Charles Firminger/Bob Bridger Collection/Online Transport Archive*

Opposite above: **Also in** operation on 10 December 1972 were ex-MSC 0-6-0T No 31 and ex-SR 'USA' 0-6-0T No 72; the pair are seen here near Oakworth with the 1.5pm service from Keighley to Oxenhope. *Charles Firminger/Bob Bridger Collection/Online Transport Archive*

Opposite below: **During the** Second World War and into the post-war years, a significant number of 'Austerity' 0-6-0STs were constructed to the design of the Hunslet Engine Co; whilst the majority were built by Hunslet in Leeds, a significant number of others were built by other manufacturers under licence. One of these other suppliers was Robert Stephenson & Hawthorns. One of these – Works No 7829 – was delivered new to the Longmoor Military Railway in July 1945; however, by this date, with war in Europe now over, the military need for locomotives was much reduced with the result that four months later the locomotive was sold to Manchester Collieries, arriving at Walkden in April the following year. Following the nationalisation of the coal industry in 1947, the locomotive, by now named *Fred*, was allocated to the National Coal Board's West Lancashire Area and saw service at Bickershaw and West Leigh collieries. In 1963 the locomotive was rebuilt; this work included the installation of an underfeed stoker and work to reduce smoke emissions based on modifications proposed by the Argentinian engineer L.D. Porta. Following withdrawal, the locomotive was preserved and arrived on the KWVR in January 1969; by this date the underfeed stoker was no longer operational and work was undertaken on the locomotive before it entered service. This included removing the underfeed stoker and repainting *Fred* into this blue livery as seen here in the spring of 1973. The locomotive was used by the KWVR for a number of years but was subsequently stored; then acquired by the Somerset & Dorset Locomotive Collection, the 0-6-0ST was moved to Tyseley for assessment in April 2003. *Roy Hobbs/Online Transport Archive*

Above: **On 19 May** 1973, when seen at Oakworth heading towards Haworth, ex-London Transport 0-6-0PT No L89 (ex-GWR/BR No 5775) is still in the livery in which it was painted for the film *The Railway Children*. The coaches behind are some of the line's ex-BR Mark 1 non-corridor suburban coaches. *Gavin Morrison*

Opposite above: **When the** line was reopened, there was no platform building at Ingrow – as shown by this view of Nos 118 *Brussels* and 41241 on an Oxenhope-bound service – and it was to be two decades before a suitable structure was erected. *John Herting/Online Transport Archive*

Opposite below: **Built by** the Leeds-based Hunslet Engine Co, Mersey Docks & Harbour Board 0-6-0DM No 32 *Huskisson* was the first diesel locomotive acquired by the board and was purchased in order to replace a fireless locomotive that had been destroyed as a result of enemy action during the Second World War. The board employed a number of fireless locomotives to serve areas of the docks – such as terminals handling oil traffic – where sparks from a conventional steam locomotive might cause accidents. By the 1960s, with the development of container traffic, the conventional docks in Liverpool were in decline and as a result the board's locomotive fleet was reduced. No 32 was withdrawn in 1970 and purchased for preservation by a KWVR member. It arrived on the line in January 1971 and is pictured here in the yard at Haworth on 14 July 1974. Initially the locomotive saw considerable use in shunting operations and on the occasional passenger train. Out of use for a number of years, the completion of its restoration coincided with the railway's diesel gala in June 2014. *Peter Watson Collection/Online Transport Archive*

Above: **On 14 April** 1974, Class 9F No 92220 *Evening Star* is pictured crossing Mytholmes Viaduct with a service towards Oxenhope. Famously the 999th and last of the BR Standard locomotives to be constructed, the '9F' emerged from Swindon Works in March 1960 having cost some £33,500 to build but only saw five years of service before withdrawal in March 1965. As the last steam locomotive constructed for BR, No 92220 was effectively scheduled for preservation from the moment it was completed. Becoming part of the future National Collection on withdrawal, No 92220 underwent a heavy overhaul at Crewe Works in early 1967 before being placed in store. The locomotive was loaned to the KWVR between July 1973 and May 1975, after which it was transferred to the new National Railway Museum at York. The locomotive is, at the time of writing, on static display at the NRM. *Peter Watson Collection/Online Transport Archive*

Opposite above: **Pictured in** the yard at Haworth on 14 April 1974 is ex-GNR six-wheeled brake third No 589. This carriage, which had been built at Doncaster in 1888, was transferred to departmental stock by the LNER by 1942 for use as a stores van. Renumbered DE940281E within the departmental listing following nationalisation, the carriage survived until accident damage in 1966 resulted in it being sent to York Works, where it was condemned. Purchased by members of the VCT for preservation, the carriage was moved as part of a parcels train from York to Bradford on 24 May 1966 and transferred to the KWVR the following day. Although at the time of writing restored externally, the VCT has plans for a further major work that will see the carriage's interior restored to original condition. *Peter Watson Collection/Online Transport Archive*

Opposite below: **On the** same day, Class 5 No 45212 is seen departing tender first from Oxenhope with a service to Keighley. The first four coaches are all non-corridor suburban coaches. The railway still possesses, at the time of writing, four of these coaches: all second No E46157; second lavatory open No E48018; composite lavatory No E43003; and brake second No E43345. A number of other examples were also owned by the railway, but these were disposed of; the underframe of all second No 46145 was used in the restoration of LYR club car No 47. *Peter Watson Collection/Online Transport Archive*

Above: **This is** the most powerful combination of steam power to work a service train on the line. BR 2-10-0 No 92220 *Evening Star* was on loan to the railway from the National Railway Museum at the time and was used on the Santa Specials together with resident ex-Swedish WD 2-8-0 No 1931. The pair is seen between Damems Loop and Oakworth on a Santa special on 22 December 1974. *Gavin Morrison*

Opposite above: **A general view** of the yard at Haworth taken on 22 March 1975 at the start of an enthusiasts' weekend. Amongst locomotives visible are Class 9F No 92220 *Evening Star* and Ivatt 2-6-2T No 41241. *Gavin Morrison*

Opposite below: **In the** late spring of 1975, ex-SJ 2-8-0 No 1931 makes an impressive sight heading towards Oxenhope. The locomotive was built by the Vulcan Foundry at Newton-le-Willows, being completed in January 1945. Shipped immediately to Europe to help with the war effort, the locomotive was sold to Nederlandse Spoorwegen (NS: Netherlands State Railways) as its No 4464. In 1953 it was sold again, this time to Statens Järnväger (SJ: Swedish State Railways) and was renumbered 1931. Withdrawn five years later, it was to spend the next fourteen years, until 1972, in store as part of SJ's strategic reserve. Preserved and repatriated to the UK, it operated as SJ No 1931 for three years before withdrawal in 1976. Work started in 1993, following an appeal launched in 1990 to raise £70,000 for the work, on its restoration to original War Department condition; this involved the removal of the modifications undertaken by SJ, including the replacement of the cab with one constructed to the original pattern, and the construction, using a salvaged eight-wheel tender chassis of a replacement tender. *Peter Watson Collection/Online Transport Archive*

Above: **Withdrawn in** 1966, BR Standard 2-6-0 No 78022 had spent almost as much time awaiting scrapping at Woodham Bros's yard at Barry – eight years – as it had in service – twelve years – when it was acquired for preservation in 1975. The condition of the locomotive is all too evident on 11 June 1975 as it is pictured arriving in the yard at Haworth. The contrast with the restored locomotive – see page 112 – is dramatic. *Gavin Morrison*

Opposite above: **During the** summer of 1975, British Rail celebrated the 150th anniversary of the Stockton & Darlington Railway with an exhibition held at Shildon between 24 and 30 August and a grand cavalcade on the 31st from Shildon to Heighington. The KWVR loaned two locomotives to the event: ex-LYR 0-4-0T No 51218 and Ivatt-designed 2-6-2T No 41241 – as seen here. The latter was the only locomotive on show that was in a non-authentic livery. *Peter Watson Collection/Online Transport Archive*

Opposite below: **Standard 2-6-4T** No 80002 is seen here in stripped down condition in Haworth yard in the late summer of 1975. Although purchased intact from BR in 1969 (No 80002 is the only surviving example of the class not to have spent time at Barry), the locomotive was in relatively poor condition on arrival having been used for carriage heating purposes at Cowlairs for a year after its withdrawal from Beattock in March 1967 and so required some remedial work before it could re-enter service. Following a complete overhaul, No 80002 was again restored to service in the 1990s; however, withdrawn in 2013 following the expiry of its most recent boiler certificate, No 80002 is now on static display at Oxenhope as the costs of a further overhaul are deemed too expensive. *Peter Watson Collection/Online Transport Archive*

Above: **Although ex-LYR** 0-4-0ST No 51218 has been a familiar sight on the line for many years, it is not the only example of the Aspinall-designed 0-4-0ST to survive in preservation. Pictured in the shed at Oxenhope in the late summer of 1975 is LYR No 19; this was one of the last of the type to be constructed at Horwich Works – in May 1910. Becoming LMS No 11243, unlike No 51218, No 11243 was destined to be a relatively early casualty, being withdrawn in 1931 and sold to the contractors John Mowlem. Amongst the projects that the locomotive was employed on was the expansion of the docks at Southampton. Sold in 1933, it passed in 1935 to the Charlton (London) based United Glass Bottle Manufacturing Ltd in 1935. Following a thirty-year life in London, it was acquired for preservation in 1967 before being purchased by the Lancashire & Yorkshire Railway Trust in 1969. However, the locomotive's condition was poor and it was only ever a static exhibit on the KWVR. Subsequently it was on display at Steamport, in Southport, and at the Preston-based Ribble Steam Railway. In January 2020 a further relocation saw the locomotive transferred to the East Lancashire Railway with work starting later that year on its possible restoration; this remains work in progress at the time of writing. *Peter Watson Collection/Online Transport Archive*

Opposite above: **Pictured in** the shed at Oxenhope in late 1975 is ex-LMS 2-6-0 No 2700. Built at Horwich in 1926 as No 13000, No 2700 was the first of the George Hughes-designed Moguls – which acquired the nickname 'Crab' – to be constructed. Although the locomotive was new, the tender was constructed on a much older underframe – indeed evidence suggests that the latter had its origins in the early 1880s. Amongst the last of the class to survive, No 42700 – as the locomotive had become after nationalisation – was withdrawn from service in March 1966 from Birkenhead shed and was preserved as part of the National Collection. Initially stored at Hellifield, No 2700 was one of a number of locomotives loaned from the National Collection to preserved railways and was moved to the Worth Valley during 1968. With minimal work it was used on passenger services although latterly was to spend its time on the railway on display. It remained on the railway until 1977 when, in the company of Class 9F No 92220, it travelled to York. Since then, the locomotive has visited a number of other preserved lines but is, at the time of writing, on static display in the National Railway Museum. *Peter Watson Collection/Online Transport Archive*

Opposite below: **Looking resplendent** in the yard at Haworth in the summer of 1977 is one of the trio of RSH-built 0-6-0STs, No 57 *Samson*. Built in 1950 (Works No 7668), No 57 was one of three of the type that arrived on the Worth Valley during May and June 1969 following their withdrawal from the ironstone lines in Northamptonshire. Outwardly similar to the Hunslet-designed 'Austerity' 0-6-0STs, the RSH-built locomotives were significantly more powerful with a tractive effort of 26,850lb as opposed to the 23,870lb of the 'Austerities'. No 57 was to survive on the Worth Valley until the early 1990s; it is now on static display on the Spa Valley Railway having donated parts, including its boiler, to the restoration of sister locomotive No 62. *Peter Watson Collection/Online Transport Archive*

Above: **In 1954,** Stewarts & Lloyds acquired two more of the RSH-built 0-6-0STs; one of these, No 63 (Works No 7761), was the first of the trio of ex-Northamptonshire ironstone locomotives to arrive on the line – in May 1969 – following withdrawal. Pictured in the yard at Haworth in the autumn of 1977 awaiting overhaul, No 63 was returned to service and remained on the line until the early 1990s. Now based on the Great Central Railway in Leicestershire, No 63's most recent overhaul was completed in December 2011 and at the time of writing the locomotive is again awaiting overhaul following the expiry of its most recent boiler certificate. *Peter Watson/ Online Transport Archive*

Opposite above: **Ivatt Atlantic** No 990 *Henry Oakley*, owned by the National Railway Museum, had been returned to working order for the 150th anniversary celebrations of the Stockton & Darlington Railway at Shildon in 1975. It was then loaned to the KWVR where it is seen at Damems loop, piloting RSH-built 0-6-0ST No 57 en route to Oxenhope, on 18 March 1978. The locomotive's sojourn on the line was shorter than anticipated as it developed boiler problems. *Gavin Morrison*

Opposite below: **In late** 1977, the railway acquired a USATC Class S160 from Polish State Railways (PKP). Pictured here at Haworth in early 1978, No TR203-474 was constructed by Lima of Ohio in the USA (Works No 8758) in 1945. Shipped to Poland to assist in the final phases of the war on the Eastern Front, the locomotive was taken over by PKP. Reboilered in 1975 but withdrawn shortly thereafter, the locomotive was originally destined for preservation in Poland but was made available to the Worth Valley. It reached the line in November 1977 and entered service, still in its Polish livery, during 1978. It was restored to its USATC guise as No 5820 for the shooting of the film *Yanks* in 1978. The locomotive's most recent overhaul was completed in early 2014 and, at the time of writing, No 5820 – nicknamed 'Big Jim' – remains part of the operational fleet. *Peter Watson Collection/Online Transport Archive*

Pictured at Keighley in early 1978 is BR Standard 4-6-0 No 75078. Completed at Swindon in January 1956, No 75078 was based on the Southern Region for its entire operational life, being allocated to Exmouth Junction, Basingstoke and Nine Elms sheds before a final transfer in May 1965 took the locomotive to Eastleigh from where it was withdrawn in July 1966. Sold initially for scrap to Woodham Bros, it was secured for preservation in early 1972. Transferred to Haworth in June that year, the locomotive, owned by the Standard 4 Locomotive Preservation Society, was restored to operational condition by early 1977. Since its initial restoration, No 75078 has had a number of further major overhauls and was expected to return to service in 2022. *Peter Watson Collection/Online Transport Archive*

INTO THE 1980s AND BEYOND

As the preserved line matured, so there was an increasing awareness of its role both as a destination in its own right and as part of a broader public transport provision. On 22 March 1980, combined bus and rail tickets from Burnley to Oxenhope were provided through the cooperation of the railway and West Yorkshire Road Car Co; these were sold at weekends and on Bank Holidays. In order to

Another ex-Woodham Bros locomotive to arrive on the railway was 'Jinty' 0-6-0T No 47279, which was purchased by the 3F Trust and arrived on the line in August 1979. Built by the Vulcan Foundry as LMS No 7119 in August 1924, the locomotive was subsequently renumbered 7279 in 1934. Based in Nottinghamshire for much of its early career, the locomotive was eventually based in Lancashire, being withdrawn from Sutton Oak shed in December 1966. Sold for scrap in 1967, it spent twelve years at Barry before being rescued and is pictured here in the yard at Haworth in early 1980, some six months after its arrival. When it made the journey north, the locomotive was in very poor condition. Restoration, which included obtaining a suitable chimney that had been originally destined to act as a flowerpot, was completed in February 1988. Since 2011, when the locomotive's most recent boiler certificate expired, No 47279 has been on static display at Oxenhope. *Peter Watson Collection/Online Transport Archive*

Like Britain, the US constructed a large number of locomotives as part of the war effort during the Second World War; many of these were shipped to Britain prior to the D-Day landings of June 1944 in preparation for the invasion whilst others were shipped directly to mainland Europe as the war progressed. One of the 2-8-0s to be shipped direct was USATC No 5820 which was constructed in 1945 by the Ohio-based Lima Locomotive Works and sent to Poland. Becoming PKP No Tr203-474, the locomotive was reboilered in 1975 shortly before it was withdrawn for preservation. Travelling by ship from Szczecin to Hull in late 1977, it arrived on the KWVR in November that year. Following minor remedial work, the locomotive entered service restored as USATC No 5820 in March the following year. The locomotive was pressed into use for the filming of *Yanks* later in 1978 and is pictured here, double-heading a train with Class 4F No 43924, in early 1980. The locomotive remained in service until 1992 and was then stored until an overhaul saw it return to service during 2014. The locomotive remains part of the line's operational fleet, although its current boiler certificate is due to expire in 2023. *Peter Watson Collection/Online Transport Archive*

promote the summer service, a single-deck bus – Burnley & Pendle Leyland National No 140 – was painted in an overall advertising livery.

The line's popularity continued to grow; ticket sales in 1981 exceeded 150,000 for the first time and represented the third year in which a record level of ticket sales had been achieved. For the next decade, passenger figures fluctuated around this level – 144,170 in 1985, 144,766 in 1986 and 156,870 in 1990. On 8 August 2007, the railway celebrated carrying its 5 millionth passenger as a preserved railway.

On 8 August 1985, No 47421 was named *The Brontës of Haworth* in a ceremony at Haworth; this was a joint venture between the Brontë Society, BR and the railway with the locomotive hauling a Pullman service to Haworth for the purpose. The locomotive, new as No D1520 in June 1963, carried the name for only a brief period – until September 1988 – and was withdrawn in September 1991. It was finally scrapped at Crewe in March 1997 after a period in store. Also in 1985, restoration of the VCT-owned *Bellerophon* was completed with the assistance of a grant from the Science Museum. The locomotive was used to haul a number of passenger services on 27, 30 and 31 December that year; these probably represented the first time that the locomotive had been used for such a purpose.

The relationship between the preserved railway and the main line developed during the course of the decade. In August 1985, the 'Steam Saver' integrated ticket was launched; this was a joint venture between the KWVR and WYPTE and was valid from any staffed WYPTE railway station for one return journey to Oxenhope. On 19 April 1986, Nos 150146 and 150114 were used on the line; this was the first use of Sprinters on any preserved line; the units had been hired by the KWVR for a special run from Chesterfield to Oxenhope.

Although recently doubts have been raised on its pedigree, for almost a century it has been accepted that *Lion* – pictured here at Keighley on 5 September 1981 – could trace its origins back to an 0-4-2 locomotive constructed by Todd, Kidson & Laird for the Liverpool & Manchester Railway (as No 57) in 1838. It was one of two similar locomotives constructed to haul freight trains that year, with a further two following in 1839. With the Liverpool & Manchester being taken over by the LNWR in 1845 – the same year in which No 57 was given a new boiler – the locomotive was renumbered 116. Withdrawn and sold in 1859, it was acquired by the Mersey Docks & Harbour Board; from 1871 it was in use as a stationary pumping engine. In 1928 it was presented to the Liverpool Engineering Society – in whose ownership it remains – and was restored for the centenary of the Liverpool & Manchester. Perhaps its most famous appearance was in the classic Ealing Comedy *The Titfield Thunderbolt*, where it was retrieved from the museum to assist in the campaign to preserve the local branch. A further restoration – in 1979 – saw the locomotive returned to steam for the 150th anniversary of the Liverpool & Manchester Railway and, the following year it, graced the KWVR's autumn steam gala. *Peter Watson Collection/Online Transport Archive*

Although the Class 8F was designed by Sir William Stanier for the LMS, wartime exigencies meant that a number of the class ordered by the Railway Executive Committee for wartime use were constructed by the other 'Big Four' companies. No 8431 was one of those completed by the GWR and emerged from Swindon Works in March 1944. Based on the Great Western until 1947, it was transferred to the LMS and initially based at Royston. Ironically, it was only to spend seven years in the West Riding before being transferred back to former GWR territory, where it was allocated to Newton Abbot, St Philip's Marsh, Old Oak Common and Bristol Barrow Road before withdrawal from Bath Green Park in January 1964. Sold to Woodham Bros seven months later, the locomotive was preserved in March 1971 and moved to the KWVR in May 1972. With restoration completed, it re-entered service in December 1975. It is pictured here departing from Keighley in the spring of 1981. Following withdrawal in 2000, No 8431 is at the time of writing on static display at Oxenhope. *Peter Watson Collection/Online Transport Archive*

In the late 1980s there was a significant change at Ingrow West. Much of this station had been demolished before the line's preservation. However, in 1985 the opportunity arose to acquire the ex-MR station building from Foulridge, on the closed line from Skipton to Colne, for £7,500 and rebuild it at Ingrow. The problem was one of funding – the overall cost of the project was £50,000 (close to £140,000 at 2022 values) – and an appeal in *Push & Pull* only resulted in a limited response. Fortunately, however, Geoffrey Reeday, whose father had been born close to Ingrow station and who was a prominent London lawyer, offered to underwrite the cost of the work. With funding guaranteed, the rebuilt station at Ingrow West was formally opened by the then Lord Lieutenant of West Yorkshire, Lord Ingrow, on 22 July 1989.

On 17 August 1988, a second locomotive was named on the line; this was No 31444 which was given the name *The Keighley & Worth Valley Railway* in a ceremony held at Keighley to mark the twentieth anniversary of the line's reopening. The Class 31 carried the name for the rest of its main line career before withdrawal at the end of 1995. A second locomotive – No 37087 – was named *The Keighley & Worth Valley Railway 40th Anniversary 1968-2008* in a ceremony at Oxenhope on 5 June 2008.

A further innovation occurred over the weekend of 5 and 6 November 1988 when the railway held its first diesel gala. Although it proved a success in some respects, the behaviour of certain enthusiasts led to complaints from a number of local residents. Having endeavoured to foster a good relationship with the communities along the valley since the line had reopened, the railway expressed its disappointment that this had been adversely affected by the mentality of a minority of those who had attended the event. Such was the concern that the organising of similar events in the future was called into question.

In 1990 the Bahamas Locomotive Society, which had previously been based at the ex-BR shed at Dinting, relocated to Ingrow using the former goods shed as a base. The decision to approve the move from Dinting to the KWVR was approved by the KWVR's

Not all locomotives acquired from the Woodham Bros scrapyard were originally slated for restoration. Ex-GWR 0-6-0PT No 4612 – which had originally been constructed at Swindon during 1942 and withdrawn from Cardiff East Dock in June 1965 – was purchased by the railway in 1981 as a source of spare parts for the line's other ex-GWR 0-6-0PT No 5775. The locomotive is seen here in the yard at Haworth on 17 April 1981 shortly after its arrival on the line. Although stripped of parts, the locomotive's remains were purchased in 1987 for restoration in the Forest of Dean. Work was completed in 2001 and the locomotive moved to the Bodmin & Wenford Railway in Cornwall. The locomotive, now owned by the Bodmin & Wenford, remains operational, having completed its most recent overhaul in 2019. *Author*

Above: **Viewed in** the yard at Haworth on 5 September 1981 is Hudswell Clarke-built 0-4-0T *Lord Mayor*. The locomotive was constructed in 1893 for Edward Nuttall to work at Salford on the construction of the docks that served the Manchester Ship Canal. During its working life, it worked on a number of construction projects in both England and Wales, being based from 1914 working on the Spurn Point Railway for the duration of the First World War. Between 1934 and 1948 it was operated by the Cliffe Hill Granite Co in Leicestershire, when it was acquired by the scrap merchant George Cohen & Co. Recognising that the 0-4-0T was a useful locomotive, it was employed by the company on a number of projects, including the dismantling of the Liverpool Overhead Railway following the closure of the 'Dockers' Umbrella' in 1957 – before being taken out of service in 1966. Presented to a trust by George Cohen & Co, *Lord Mayor* reached the KWVR in June 1968. The locomotive was acquired by the VCT in 1990 and, at the time of writing, is on display at the trust's museum at Ingrow. *Peter Watson Collection/Online Transport Archive*

Opposite above: **The KWVR** is home to a number of ex-LYR locomotives. No 752 was originally built as an 0-6-0 tender locomotive to the design of William Barton Wright and built at Beyer, Peacock in May 1881 as one of the 280-strong Class 25 built between 1876 and 1887. Of these, all bar fifty were rebuilt to the design of John Aspinall into 0-6-0STs as the LYR needed additional shunting locomotives. No 752 was rebuilt at Horwich in 1896. Becoming LMS No 11496, the locomotive was withdrawn in 1937 and sold. Passing to the Coppull (Lancashire) based Blainscough Colliery Co, No 752 became part of the National Coal Board's fleet on Nationalisation in 1947; stored in the open in 1958 at Parsonage Colliery the locomotive was in poor condition when acquired for preservation nine years later. Largely restored before moving to the KWVR in late 1971, No 752 entered service in May 1972. Later in the decade No 752 was overhauled before appearing at the Liverpool & Manchester 150th celebrations at Rainhill during 1980. When recorded crossing Mytholmes Viaduct, the locomotive was approaching the end of its initial operational life on the KWVR. Withdrawn in 1982, the locomotive was partially dismantled at Haworth, a condition it remained in for almost a quarter of a century before it was moved to the East Lancashire Railway in mid-2016. Restoration of the locomotive, owned by the Lancashire & Yorkshire Railway Trust, was completed in 2020. Although now based on the East Lancashire Railway, an agreement exists for the locomotive to make periodic visits to the KWVR. *Peter Watson Collection/Online Transport Archive*

On 6 March 1982, the sole surviving Edward Thompson-designed Class K1 No 2005 – a number that it never carried in service as it was completed as BR No 62005 in June 1949 – arrived at Keighley after it had operated the 'Trans-Pennine Pullman' special from Carnforth to Leeds. The 'K1' was then to spend three weeks operating on the Worth Valley – including an appearance at the railway's spring Enthusiasts' Weekend (27/28 March) – before returning to its home on the North Yorkshire Moors Railway on Monday 29 March. It is seen here crossing Mytholmes Viaduct with an Oxenhope-bound service double-heading with one of the trio of ex-Stewarts & Lloyds RSH-built 0-6-0STs. *Peter Watson Collection/ Online Transport Archive*

One of the more unusual vehicles to have operated over the line in preservation was British Rail's LEV1, which was the result of a project between BR and British Leyland to produce low-cost railcars to replace the ageing first-generation DMUs. The forerunner of the later Classes 141 and 142, LEV1 is seen here at Oxenhope in July 1982. *Harry Luff/Online Transport Archive*

Railway Council at a meeting held on 11 April 1990. In addition to bringing the 'Jubilee' class 4-6-0 No 5596 *Bahamas* to the Worth Valley, the society was also the custodian of the sole surviving LNWR 'Coal Tank' – No 1054 – which had been donated to the National Trust in 1963 and placed on loan with the Society a decade later (the locomotive had been on loan previously to the railway during June and July 1986 when it was used on a number of special services). The society now operates the goods shed at Ingrow partly as a workshop and partly as a museum that houses its own collection; the museum at the time of writing accommodates two of the society's locomotives – Hudswell Clarke & Co 0-6-0T No 1704 *Nunlow* and Andrew Barclay 0-4-0ST No 2258 *Tiny* (the latter was originally named *R. Walker* when employed by the Manchester Corporation Gas Department at its Bradford Road, Manchester, works).

Also in 1990, the turntable was installed at Keighley station. This had been purchased in February 1988 and had been previously installed at Garsdale on the Settle to Carlisle

After a ceremony held to mark the return of 'West Country' No 34092 *City of Wells* to running order held on 1 April 1980, the locomotive is seen climbing out of Keighley station. It carries the 'Golden Arrow' embellishments that it carried frequently when it was allocated to Stewarts Lane and used on the prestigious Pullman service from Victoria to Dover. Completed at Brighton in September 1949 and originally named *Wells* – it became *City of Wells* in March 1950 – No 34092 was allocated new to the South Eastern Division of the Southern. Following electrification of Kent coast services, the locomotive was reallocated to the South Western Division, being withdrawn in November 1964. Sold to Woodham Bros, it was at Barry from March 1965 until October 1971. Purchased by some members of the KWVR, No 34092's restoration was completed in 1979. Withdrawn in 1989 on the expiry of its boiler certificate, it was not until 2014 that No 34092 was returned to operation. The following year, during a move by road for an appearance on the Gloucestershire Warwickshire Railway, a weight check indicated that the transporter with locomotive was over the permitted axle loadings. This discovery led the City of Bradford Metropolitan District Council to impose a temporary weight restriction on a road bridge at Ingrow; it was over this bridge that locomotive movements to and from the line were made and the restriction – subsequently lifted – meant that it was impossible for No 34092 to return to the KWVR following its loan. As a result, the locomotive was temporarily transferred to the East Lancashire Railway; this arrangement became permanent in March 2019 when the locomotive was purchased by the ELR. *Gavin Morrison*

line. When new in 1884 it had cost £200. However, the transfer of the turntable to the line was delayed temporarily due to opposition from the Yorkshire Dales National Park Committee, which had sought to get it listed in its original position. Following its installation at Keighley, the turntable received a Special Commendation in that year's Restored Stations competition; the goods shed at Oakworth received a Highly Commended in the same competition. The turntable underwent a major overhaul in 2014.

Above: **Built by** the Haydock Foundry in 1874, the 0-6-0WT *Bellerophon* was designed by Josiah Evans, whose father owned collieries and engineering businesses to the east of Liverpool. The locomotive was one of six constructed in the company's workshops for use on the company's colliery lines. Although generally limited to these lines, as a result of running powers that the Evans family claimed over the LYR and LNWR, the six locomotives could also be found on the main line, including hauling passenger trains for the use of the company's employees to and from Blackpool. As a result of the nationalisation of the coal industry in 1947, all six passed to the National Coal Board but were withdrawn by the early 1960s. *Bellerophon* is the sole survivor; preserved in 1964, it was presented to the KWVR. However, little work was undertaken on the locomotive until it was sold – for a token sum – to the VCT in 1981. With funds raised for its restoration, the locomotive was returned to an operational condition and is seen here, after restoration, in Keighley during the spring of 1986. Whilst remaining in the ownership of the VCT, *Bellerophon* is too small a locomotive to be operated on the Worth Valley and so has been based for a number of years on the Foxfield Railway in Staffordshire. It is currently out of use again, its boiler certificate having expired at the end of 2018. *Peter Watson Collection/Online Transport Archive*

Opposite above: **The Austerity** 0-6-0ST was produced in significant numbers between 1943 and 1964, mainly by its designer (the Leeds-based Hunslet Engine Co) but with a significant number also produced by other manufacturers. War Department No 118 *Brussels* was one of 50 constructed by Hudswell Clarke and was completed – as War Department No 71505 – in March 1945. Allocated to the Longmoor Military Railway from new, the locomotive was to be based at the line for its entire working life. Damaged in an accident in June 1953, it was returned to service in May 1958 following rebuilding at Hunslet. Subsequently, the locomotive was converted to oil firing; it was withdrawn in 1967, still fitted for oil firing, and preserved in January 1969 at Liphook. The closure of the Longmoor Military Railway led to an ill-fated attempt to preserve the line and No 118 returned to its home briefly. The failure of the Longmoor project resulted in the locomotive being sold. It arrived on the Worth Valley in September 1971. Initially, the locomotive was found not to perform well but, with modification and the use of lighter grade oil, operation improved. No 118 was withdrawn in 1988, following the expiry of its boiler certificate, and remains on the railway on static display. *Harry Luff/Online Transport Archive*

In the 1980s, British Rail named a number of main line locomotives after the country's most successful preserved railways. One of the lines so recognised was the Worth Valley with Class 31 No 31444 being named *Keighley & Worth Valley Railway* in August 1988. The locomotive, bearing its then new nameplate, is seen here at Doncaster depot on 15 September 1988. The locomotive, new originally as No D5555 in October 1959, had initially become No 31137 under the TOPS renumbering; between May 1990 and January 1994, it carried the number 31544 and was withdrawn, as No 31444, in December 1995. After a period in store, the locomotive was cut up at Wigan in March 2001. *Gavin Morrison*

The mighty 'Deltic' Class 55 diesel-electrics have visited the line for galas. Here on 5 November 1988, No 55015 *Tulyar* is seen pulling out of Keighley for Oxenhope during the line's first diesel gala. In the distance can be seen a Class 24 awaiting its next duty.
Gavin Morrison

THE LAST THIRTY YEARS

By 1990 the Worth Valley had matured into a well-established preserved railway; in many respects, whilst much has happened over the past 30 years, these developments are – for the most part – similar to what had been evolving over the previous decade. Inheriting a complete railway with most of its stations intact was both a strength and a potential weakness for the line; its very completeness meant that it lacked the major projects that other lines have had – such as the return to East Grinstead on the Bluebell Railway – and there is undoubtedly much less romance – and profile – in maintenance than in these more grandiose schemes. I have, therefore, deliberately decided to cease the detailed narrative at 1990 but explore some aspects of the period since then through photographs; these recall some of the locomotives that have appeared on special events and other aspects of the line's recent history.

On the occasion of the line's first diesel gala – on 5 November 1988 – Class 25 No D5209 is seen descending the bank towards Keighley station. Work started on the construction of No D5209 in March 1963 at Derby Works with the completed locomotive entering service in late June 1963. Initially allocated to the LMR, the Class 25, which became No 25059 under the TOPS renumbering scheme, was to see service on both Western and Scottish regions before it ended its career once again allocated to the LMR. It spent the last five years of its operational life based at Crewe, from where it was withdrawn in March 1987. Stored until early July 1987, when it was moved by rail to Leicester, No 25059 was transferred to the scrapyard operated by Vic Berry, where many other members of the class were disposed of, before being purchased for preservation in September 1987. The cost of purchase was £9,384.28 (plus VAT) with the additional sum of £1,500 (plus VAT) for the removal of asbestos. Early the following month it was moved, again by rail (at a cost of £1,400 plus VAT), to the KWVR where it was to become the first main-line diesel to be based on the line and entered service in late October 1987. The locomotive is, at the time of writing, out of service awaiting an overhaul with work complicated by damage wrought by the floods caused by Storm Ciara on 8/9 February 2020. *Gavin Morrison*

Ex-Furness Railway
No 20, built originally by Sharp, Stewart, is the oldest working standard-gauge steam locomotive in Britain. After a long career, it was finally withdrawn in 1960 but was not actually preserved until 1983. A full restoration commenced in the late 1990s and the locomotive entered service at the Lakeside & Haverthwaite Railway in 1999. It is seen here, fully restored, at Keighley shortly after the restoration work was completed. *Harry Luff/Online Transport Archive*

No 20 formed a train with two preserved ex-Metropolitan Railway carriages – No 427 and, closest to the camera, No 465 – that date from 1910 and 1919 respectively. One of the facets of the KWVR is the impressive collection of historic coaching stock that is based on the line. *Harry Luff/Online Transport Archive*

On 2 February 1992 ex-GWR 0-6-0PT No 5775, which had been repainted into BR green livery the previous year having spent the previous thirty years either in LT or non-authentic liveries, is pictured at Oxenhope in BR livery. Completed at Swindon in September 1929, the locomotive was transferred to Carmarthen in October 1952 and then Pontypool Road in March 1956; it was withdrawn from the latter in mid-January 1963. This was not, however, to be the end of No 5775's operational career; one of twelve 0-6-0PTs to be transferred from BR to the London Transport Executive, No 5775 officially became part of the LT fleet in July 1963 as No L89. The locomotive was purchased for preservation in January 1970 and transferred to the KWVR. Used in the filming of *The Railway Children*, the locomotive – now out of use and requiring a major overhaul – was repainted into the livery it wore for the film. This was initially for an exhibition at the National Railway Museum, but it remains on display at Oxenhope in this condition. *Gavin Morrison*

The 228-strong Class 20 Bo-Bo diesel-electrics represented one of the earliest and also most successful of the Modernisation Plan locomotives introduced to BR service in the late 1950s. No D8031 – pictured here in the yard at Haworth in the late spring of 2000 – was constructed at Darlington Works and entered service in January 1960 and was to see more than thirty years' service prior to withdrawal in September 1990. Allocated to the Scottish Region when new, it was transferred to England in June 1968, being allocated to a number of depots, including Stratford, York and Gateshead, before withdrawal from Toton. Purchased by a group of KWVR volunteers, the locomotive has at the time of writing been based on the Worth Valley, where it arrived in August 1992, almost as long as its operational main-line career. *Harry Luff/Online Transport Archive*

Above: **During the** 1950s and early 1960s, BR acquired a significant number of diesel shunters, often in small numbers, from various contractors. As the railways contracted, however, many of these designs were deemed to be non-standard and thus destined for a relatively short main-line career. Such was the fate of the ten 0-6-0 diesel mechanical shunters – Nos D2510-19 – that were supplied by Hudswell Clarke to the LMR between August and November 1961. All were withdrawn by the end of 1967 with six being scrapped quickly thereafter. Four, however, were to be purchased by the NCB. One of this quartet was No D2511, which had been employed by BR at the docks at Barrow and Worthington, which was used by the NCB at Brodsworth Colliery near Doncaster. Withdrawn in 1977 following accident damage, the locomotive was purchased for use on the Worth Valley, arriving on the line in August 1977. It entered service three years later. The railway also purchased sister No D2519 in April 1982; this locomotive was, however, destined to be used as a source of spare parts and was eventually scrapped at Keighley by Marple & Gillott in March 1985. *Harry Luff/Online Transport Archive*

Opposite above: **Between 1863** and 1866, Sharp, Stewart & Co supplied eight 0-4-0 locomotives to the Furness Railway; however, the growing traffic that the railway carried soon rendered these locomotives inadequate and, in 1870, six were sold to the Barrow Haematite Steel Co. Before delivery, the sextet was rebuilt by Sharp, Stewart into 0-4-0STs, with No 20 becoming the company's No 7. In 1960, when the company's operations were dieselised, two of the ex-Furness Railway locomotives were still extant; these were given to local schools for display. No 7 survived in this role for some twenty years, until the school's relocation, when it was purchased for preservation. Passing to the Furness Railway Trust in 1990, the locomotive was restored to original condition, aided by a significant Heritage Lottery Fund grant, and was formally relaunched on 20 April 1999. The newly restored locomotive, at the time the country's oldest working standard gauge steam locomotive, was loaned to the KWVR for the railway's steam gala on 13/14 May 2000. Limited to operating a two-coach shuttle between Keighley and Ingrow, the locomotive is pictured here in Keighley during the event. The second of the two ex-FR locomotives that survived to 1960, Furness No 25, also survives; it is intended that this locomotive be restored in its 0-4-0ST guise. *Harry Luff/Online Transport Archive*

Opposite below: **It is** early 2001 and the snow gives the yard at Haworth a picturesque feel as one of the line's preserved first-generation DMUs stands alongside visiting Taff Vale Railway No 85. Designed by Tom Hurry Riches, the Taff Vale's Class O2 0-6-2T was built by the Glasgow-based Neilson, Reid & Co Ltd. No 85, new in 1899, was the first of the nine-strong class to be delivered. All nine passed to the GWR in 1922, when the Taff Vale was taken over by its larger competitor, but as non-standard were soon to be withdrawn; all were taken out of service between 1926 and 1928. No 85 – as GWR No 426 – was sold in 1929 to the Lambton, Hetton & Joicey Colliery Co in County Durham. Surviving to be nationalised with the coal industry and latterly based at Philadelphia Colliery as No 52, the locomotive remained in service until dieselisation in 1968. Initially preserved by the Midland & Great Northern Railway Preservation Society, it was sold to the KWVR before it had moved from the colliery. It arrived on the KWVR in December 1970. Although largely in original condition, four decades in industry had led to minor modifications and restoration of the locomotive in the 1990s saw it returned to its original condition. Taken out of service in 2010, the locomotive's overhaul was completed in 2016 and, at the time of writing, No 85 remains part of the line's operational fleet. *Vintage Carriages Trust/Online Transport Archive*

Above: **The ex-Lancashire** & Yorkshire Railway 0-6-0, restored to BR condition as No 52044, is seen outside the shed at Haworth in the spring of 2002 shortly after a six-year restoration project was completed. Designed by Barton Wright, a total of 280 of the LYR's Class 25 0-6-0s were constructed between 1876 and 1887; however, the introduction of the later – and more powerful – Class 27 in 1889 resulted in all but the most recent fifty of the Class 25s being rebuilt as 0-6-0STs between 1891 and 1900. Of the remaining fifty, twenty-five survived to be passed to BR on 1 January 1948 but all bar one of these had been withdrawn by the end of 1955. The final survivor – LYR No 957, LMS No 12044 and BR No 52044 (which had been built by Beyer, Peacock & Co Ltd in 1887) – soldiered on for a further three years before withdrawal in June 1959 from Wakefield shed. By this date there was interest in the locomotive's preservation from Tony Cox. Initially, however, he struggled to raise the £1,250 required to purchase the locomotive and there was a real threat that it might be scrapped. Taking out a loan for the balance, the locomotive's future was secured in early 1960. Stored for a period at Retford, it arrived on the KWVR in March 1965. Used by the railway both on passenger services and for filming – most notably in *The Railway Children* of 1971 which resulted in its nickname (the 'Green Dragon') – the locomotive was withdrawn in 1975 and was not to operate again for more than a quarter of a century. Following its return in 2002, it saw a further decade of use before withdrawal again in 2013. At the time of writing, the locomotive is being overhauled for a return to service. *Vintage Carriages Trust/Online Transport Archive*

Opposite above: **When the** line was preserved, the KWVR inherited buildings at most of the stations; the major exception, however, was at Ingrow where the original MR structure had been demolished. In 1985, the opportunity arose to purchase and relocate the similar MR station building at Foulridge on the closed line from Skipton to Colne. Although an appeal in *Push & Pull* had only a limited success in raising the then £50,000 required for the work, the KWVR was fortunate that a benefactor – the late Geoffrey Reeday – was prepared to fund the work. The rebuilt building – seen here in 2004 – was officially opened by Lord Ingrow, the Lord Lieutenant of West Yorkshire. *Robin Leleux*

Opposite below: **A scene that** demonstrates the success of the K&WVR in recreating the railway of the late 1950s or early 1960s; a preserved two-car DMU is pictured in Keighley station in the spring of 2005. The train is formed of Class 108 Nos 50928 and 51565. Based on experience with the earlier lightweight units constructed at Derby Works in the early 1950s, a total of 333 Class 108 coaches were constructed between 1958 and 1961; the pair preserved on the KWVR – which formed a two-car set when delivered to Llandudno Junction following construction at Derby in November 1959 – were both in service for more than thirty years – albeit not always operating together – until withdrawn in March 1992; No 50928 ran, from September 1984, as No 53928. At the time of writing, the set is currently out of traffic and stored at Haworth awaiting overhaul. *Vintage Carriages Trust/Online Transport Archive*

'Jubilee' class
4-6-0 No
5690 *Leander* waits
to depart from
Keighley with a
service in late 2006.
*Vintage Carriages
Trust/Online
Transport Archive*

The diminutive
station at Damems
recorded in June
2008; the platform
is barely the length
of a single coach,
the station has been
the recipient of a
number of awards
over the years. These
include winning the
British Rail Award at
the National Railway
Heritage Awards in
1995. *Robin Leleux*

Another station that has regularly received awards over the years is Oakworth; although this view was taken in 2010, such is the quality of the work in restoring and maintaining the building that it could have been taken at almost any era in the station's long life. It epitomises perfectly the skill of the KWVR in recreating the ambience of the line's branch line history. *Robin Leleux*

The only Class 31 to be painted in EWS livery and run on Network Rail was No 31466, which visited the line for the 2012 diesel gala. It is shown heading for Oxenhope just past Haworth Yard on 20 May 2012. *Gavin Morrison*

Above: **The 309-strong** Type 3 (later Class 37) locomotives were designed and manufactured by English Electric either at its Vulcan Foundry Works or subcontracted to Robert Stephenson & Hawthorns Ltd at their works at Darlington; No D6775, renumbered 37075 as part of the TOPS scheme, was to emerge from the latter in September 1962. Initially based at Hull (Dairycoates), the locomotive was allocated to a number of sheds, including March, Stratford, Thornaby and Tinsley, during a career that lasted more than thirty years. Stored in 1994, the locomotive became part of the EWS fleet in 1998 before being preserved in 1999. Based on the Great Central, Ecclesbourne Valley and Churnet Valley railways, No 37075 finally reached the KWVR in 2012 when it was acquired by a number of the line's volunteers. It is seen here in the yard at Haworth on 26 May 2012 in blue livery shortly after its arrival. *Gavin Morrison*

Opposite above: **On 3 November** 2012, a rare visitor to the line came in the form of East Midlands Trains' HST on a charity special from St Pancras. No 43082 is seen at the head of the train at Haworth station en route to Oxenhope. Notice how the vegetation has grown since the view of the Peckett seen earlier! Given the line's involvement with the filming of the Lionel Jeffries' version of *The Railway Children* (and the earlier BBC television series based on the same book), the fact that the power car is named *The Railway Children* – after the charity that supports street and vulnerable children found at railway stations – is appropriate. Following withdrawal, No 43082 was secured for preservation by 125 Heritage Ltd and is, at the time of writing, based on the Colne Valley Railway in Essex. *Gavin Morrison*

Opposite below: **On 9 March** 2014, Hudswell Clarke & Co Ltd 0-6-0T No 1704 *Nunlow* is seen at Oxenhope having just arrived with a Down train. The locomotive, which was new in 1938, was delivered new to the cement manufacturers G. & T. Earle (later part of Associated Portland Cement [APC]) for use on the company's works in Derbyshire. Named after one of the hills that formed part of the quarry and works complex, it operated over the two-mile branch that linked the works with the Manchester to Sheffield line at Hope. Although fitted with a new copper firebox as late as 1960 during a major overhaul, the locomotive was stored in 1964 as diesel traction took over. Four years later the locomotive was offered for sale and was purchased by the *Bahamas* Locomotive Society and moved to Dinting during the spring of 1969 and first steamed in preservation during April that year. Transferred as part of the society's collection to the KWVR in 1990 (following a brief stint on the Swanage Railway), *Nunlow* was restored to operational condition in 2008. Its most recent boiler certificate expired in 2018 and the locomotive is at the time of writing awaiting overhaul and on display in the museum at Ingrow. *Gavin Morrison*

Above: **The substantial** water tank at the country end of platform 4 at Keighley pictured on 3 June 2014. *Author*

Opposite above: **On 3 June** 2014, 'Austerity' 2-8-0 No 90733 runs round its train at Keighley station. Designed by Robert A. Riddles, the 'Austerity' locomotives were built for operation during the Second World War; although a number of the 2-8-0 design were to see service with Britain's railways post-war, none of those that survived with BR were preserved on withdrawal. Following the decision to return ex-SJ No 1931 to its original WD condition, the restored locomotive was officially relaunched on 23 July 2007 bearing the next number following on from those allocated to the BR locomotives (the last of the 733 operated by BR being No 90732). The locomotive is, at the time of writing, again out of service following the expiry of its boiler certificate with its overhaul being a work in progress. *Author*

Opposite below: **The yard** at Haworth on 3 June 2014; the contrast between this scene and those of five decades ago is remarkable. Apart from the construction of the shed, which provides covered accommodation for the operational fleet, the presence of three types of diesel – Classes 08, 20 and 25 – is indicative of how preservation has evolved since the railway's rebirth in the late 1960s. Diesel galas are now as much a part of the railway's calendar as steam operation and bring non-steam enthusiasts to the line. The '08' – No 08266 – is one of two based on the line at the time of writing, the other being No 08993 (one of those that was cut down for use on the Burry Port & Gwendraeth Valley line in south Wales). No 08266 was built at Darlington and delivered new as No 13336 (later No D3336) to Darnall shed in Sheffield during February 1957. Apart from a one-year sojourn in London – between May 1957 and May 1958 – when it was based at King's Cross, the locomotive was to spend the bulk of its career allocated to sheds in Sheffield although it was finally withdrawn from Shirebrook in March 1985. No 08993, new as No D3759 (and later No 08592), was constructed at Crewe Works in October 1959 and was a Western Region locomotive for its entire working career. Reduced in height for use on the BP&GV in the mid-1980s. Following the line's closure in the late 1990s, No 08993 was one of three of the sub-class to be employed, before preservation, on construction work on extensions to the Manchester Metrolink system during the first decade of the twenty-first century. *Author*

Above: **Viewed from** a Down train in 2014 the quality of the workmanship in the rebuilt station at Ingrow is clearly evident. In the background can be seen the shed occupied by the VCT. *Author*

Opposite above: **Designed by** Francis Webb, LNWR No 1054 – pictured here in Keighley station on 30 August 2014 – was completed at Crewe Works in September 1888. It was one of a class of 300 0-6-2T 'Coal Tanks' constructed for the railway between 1881 and 1897; withdrawal of the type commenced in 1921 and 291 examples passed to the LMS in 1923 and sixty-four to BR on 1 January 1948. Withdrawal of the class was rapid, with only five being in service at the end of 1954 and one alone – No 58926 (as No 1054 had become following nationalisation) – a year later. This sole survivor, which was used to haul (along with 'Super D' 0-8-0 No 49121) the last train on the Abergavenny to Merthyr line (in January 1958), was withdrawn in November 1958. Destined initially for scrap, an appeal resulted in the locomotive's preservation and restoration to LNWR livery. Ownership passed to the National Trust in 1963 with No 1054 being placed on display at Penrhyn Castle in North Wales until 1973 when the locomotive was lent to the *Bahamas* Locomotive Society and transferred to Dinting. Following restoration, which permitted its appearance at the celebrations held at Rainhill to mark the 150th anniversary of the Liverpool & Manchester Railway, No 1054 spent time both on the main line and on a number of preserved lines (including the KWVR in 1986), before being transferred to the KWVR with the rest of the BLS collection in 1990. The locomotive is, at the time of writing, towards the end of a further overhaul that was scheduled to see No 1054 returned to service during 2022. *Gavin Morrison*

Opposite below: **On 6 May** 2019 Class 37 No 37075, by now repainted into grey, is seen on the loop at Haworth with a service towards Keighley. The 1,750bhp locomotive is the most powerful diesel locomotive currently resident on the line. *Gavin Morrison*

Above: **A stark contrast** to the condition in which it arrived on the line in 1975 this view records the BR Standard 2-6-0 No 78022 piloting visiting Class 31 No 97205 on the loop at Haworth on 6 May 2019. No 78022, one of a class of sixty-five built between December 1952 and November 1956 (and one of three of the type to survive in preservation; a fourth – No 78059 – is being used as the basis of the construction of 2-6-2T No 84030 on the Bluebell Railway), was completed at Darlington Works in May 1954. It spent its early career allocated to the Eastern Region, before being transferred to the LMR in December 1962; it was withdrawn from Lostock Hall in September 1966 and was sold to Woodham Bros. Arriving at the scrapyard in March 1967, preservation came in 1975 when it was purchased by the same group that owns No 75078. It was not, however, until 1981 that work on restoration commenced; following a decade of work, including the construction of a new tender tank, No 78022 returned to service in 1991. Displayed statically from 2000, following the expiry of its boiler certificate, work on No 78022's overhaul commenced in 2015 with work being completed in late 2018. At the time of writing, No 78022 remains part of the KWVR's operational fleet. *Gavin Morrison*

Opposite above: **The spring** of 2020 brought the Coronavirus to the United Kingdom; this is not the place to examine the history of the country's response to the virus, but it did have serious consequences both for the National Network and for preserved railways. The series of lockdowns and varying layers of restrictions on what was permissible meant that travel by rail plummeted and the threat to the future of many of the preserved lines – including the Worth Valley – was in doubt as income effectively dried up. Although there were various government grants and loans available, any means of generating income had to be explored and this led to the sight, seen here on 23 May 2020, of eighteen of Northern's Class 144 units being stored at Keighley. The class, already scheduled for withdrawal later in the year, were effectively rendered surplus to requirements when main line passenger services were radically reduced and, with no spare capacity to store them elsewhere, storage at Keighley provided the railway with a useful source of income at a time when it was impossible to operate services. The financial position of the railway had already been adversely affected by flooding at Haworth caused by Storm Ciara in February 2020. Of the two units closest to the camera in this view, No 144022 was preserved by the Keith & Dufftown Railway and moved by road to Scotland on 4 September 2020 whilst No 144012, which had been subject to modification in early 2015 as a trial to see if it was possible to upgrade the class to cater for improved disabled access, was sold to Network Rail in 2021. *Gavin Morrison*

Through the generosity of the leasing company Porterbrook, one of the withdrawn Class 144 'Pacers', No 144011, was donated to the Worth Valley on 26 June 2020. The Class 144 units, which had been built by Walter Alexander on underframes supplied by BR, was procured for operation on services supported by West Yorkshire PTE and entered service during 1986 and 1987. When new, the class was allocated to Neville Hill in Leeds and saw service, before the routes were electrified, to Ilkley and Skipton and so were a regular sight at Keighley for a number of years. In later years, the type's area of operation altered with their later career being predominantly in South Yorkshire. Although destined for withdrawal in 2019, late deliveries of new rolling stock meant a temporary reprieve; this was, however, cut short as a result of reduced requirements following the arrival of Coronavirus in spring 2020. Here No 144011 is seen before withdrawal passing the ex-MR Ilkley Junction signal box on 15 May 1993. *Gavin Morrison*

VINTAGE CARRIAGES TRUST

The origins of the Trust date back to the mid-1960s and the early days of the line's preservation. A group of volunteers, with a particular interest in historic wooden-bodied coaching stock, decided to attempt the preservation of historic coaching stock. At the time there was a considerable number of historic coaches still serving the railway industry – primarily in departmental use – but as the railways contracted and as more modern rolling stock became available for this departmental work, so the numbers rapidly declined. There was also concern that, being wooden bodied, preserved examples would not survive well being stored in the open as well as the ever-present threat of damage from vandalism.

The VCT became a registered charity in 1981 and over the years has developed the yard at Ingrow to provide both museum and restoration facilities. The first phase of the Ingrow Carriage Museum opened in 1990 with a substantial extension being completed seven years later; this was formally opened in 1998.

The quality of the restoration work undertaken on the collection is evinced both by the number of awards that have been received and by the regular use of the collection in filming for both television and film. Carriages from the trust have appeared in such notable series as *Brideshead Revisited* as well as numerous episodes of the classic Granada-produced series of adaptations of the Sherlock Holmes stories starring Jeremy Brett.

The VCT collection is now on display in the Museum of Rail Travel. The collection includes three industrial locomotives that all have a long connection with the railway. These are the 0-6-0WT *Bellerophon* built by Haydock Foundry in 1876, the Manning Wardle-built 0-6-0ST *Sir Berkeley* of 1899 (Works No 1210) and the Hudswell Clarke-built 0-4-0ST *Lord Mayor* of 1893 (Works No 402). Of these *Bellerophon* is, at the time of writing, on loan to the Foxfield Railway in Staffordshire whilst *Sir Berkeley* is operational following the acquisition of a new boiler in 2006 and is on loan to the Middleton Railway in Leeds. *Lord Mayor* is at present on display in a non-operable condition in the museum. Alongside the steam locomotives, the trust also now owns one of the two Waggon und Maschinenbau diesel railbuses – No 79962 – that were based on the railway from the late 1960s. New in 1958, the railbus has retained its original Büssing engine; these were problematic in BR service and the other surviving Waggon und Maschinenbau unit – No 79964 – was fitted with a replacement AEC unit. The railbus was acquired from the railway in 2014; No 79962 is currently under restoration and on static display at Ingrow.

The Trust's collection also includes nine historic carriages, many of which have connections back to the earliest days of the branch's preservation. These are MSLR four-wheel tri-composite No 176 (built at Gorton in 1876), MR six-wheel composite No 358 (built at Derby in 1886), GNR six-wheel brake third No 589 (built at Doncaster in 1888), GNR lavatory composite brake No 2856 (built at Doncaster in 1898), the three ex-Metropolitan carriages (compartment brake third No 427 [1910], compartment third No 565 [1919] and compartment first No 509 [1923]), Southern Railway corridor 'Matchboard' brake No 3554 (built by the Metropolitan Carriage, Wagon & Finance

Company of Birmingham to a design of the South Eastern & Chatham Railway) and Bulleid-designed BR open third No S1469S (built in November 1950). All are, at the time of writing, based on the railway with the exception of No S1469S, which is on long-term loan to the Embsay & Bolton Abbey Steam Railway.

The VCT's vintage train was first operated during April and May 1991; it proved an immediate success with some 1,700 passengers willing to pay the £1 supplement to travel on the set.

BAHAMAS LOCOMOTIVE SOCIETY

Formed to preserve the 'Jubilee' class 4-6-0 No 45596 *Bahamas* following its withdrawal in July 1966 from Stockport Edgeley shed, the society was originally based at the Dinting Railway Centre. The society leased the ex-GCR shed, which originally dated to 1894 and which had been closed by BR in 1954 following the electrification of the Manchester-Sheffield via Woodhead line, to accommodate the 'Jubilee' as well as other preserved steam locomotives. In 1990, the centre was closed and the collection relocated to Ingrow on the KWVR where the society occupied the former goods shed. The shed now forms two functions; part is used as a workshop for the maintenance of the society's collection and the remainder acts as a museum. The shed is part of the Rail Story at Ingrow; this feature of the railway includes the two museums – those of the BLS and the VCT – along with the rebuilt station and a learning coach. The BLS collection includes, as well as the 'Jubilee', the only surviving ex-LNWR 'Coal Tank' No 1054 which is on long-term loan from the National Trust, the Hudswell Clarke & Co-built No 1704 *Nunlow*, the Andrew Barclay-built 0-4-0T No 2258 *Tiny* that was used by Manchester Corporation and the Robert Stephenson & Hawthorn-built crane tank *Southwick*.

Following withdrawal from Stockport Edgeley shed in July 1966, 'Jubilee' class No 45596 *Bahamas* was purchased for preservation by the Bahamas Locomotive Society in January 1967. The locomotive was then overhauled at the Leeds-based Hunslet Engine Co, where work was completed in the spring of 1968. Following the signing of a lease later that year, the locomotive was moved to the ex-GCR shed at Dinting – where it is pictured on 4 October 1969 – which was to be its base for the next two decades. The small one-road GCR shed was opened in 1894; closed originally in 1935, it was re-opened in 1942. Final closure came in 1954 with the completion of the electrification of the Woodhead route. The Bahamas Locomotive Society occupied the shed until 1990. More than three decades on the shed is still extant, albeit now surrounded by verdant woodland. *Chris Gammell/Online Transport Archive*

LANCASHIRE & YORKSHIRE RAILWAY TRUST

First established as the L&YR Saddletanks Fund in 1964 and renamed in 1987 as the Lancashire & Yorkshire Railway Preservation Society, in 1991 it became the Lancashire & Yorkshire Trust when it became a registered charity. The trust owns three locomotives – the two 0-4-0ST 'Pugs' Nos 51218 and 19 and 0-6-0ST

A reminder of the classic Lionel Jeffries' version of *The Railway Children* in the shed at Oxenhope on 3 June 2014. In the centre is Jenny Agutter with fellow stars Sally Thomsett and Gary Warren. Ironically, of the three 'children', Sally Thomsett was twenty, two years older than Jenny Agutter, when the film was shot and considerable efforts were made to disguise the fact with the result that whilst Agutter was treated as an adult, Thomsett was regarded by the crew as being much closer to the eleven-year-old that she was portraying. On the left is ex-LYR Hughes-designed bogie brake third No 1474. This was originally built at Newton Heath in 1910 for use on transpennine express services between Leeds, Bradford and Liverpool, the carriage ended its days in departmental use before acquired for preservation in 1965. Initially based at Haworth where, following a limited amount of work, it was used as volunteer accommodation – nicknamed the 'Haworth Hilton' – it was transferred to Oxenhope in the early 1970s where a full restoration programme commenced. This was completed in May 1993. Since then further work has been undertaken to ensure the carriage's preservation; at the time of writing a major project to complete work on the chassis and bogies, undertaken by the East Lancashire Railway, is approaching completion. *Author*

No 752 – along with four restored carriages. These are Club Carriage No 47, six-wheel four-compartment first No 279, bogie five-compartment brake third No 1474 and six-wheel five-compartment third No 1507. Whilst the coaches and No 51218 are based on the Worth Valley, the other two locomotives are currently on the East Lancashire where restoration work has been undertaken. The trust recently took over ownership of the body of six-wheel saloon No 12 although this is in storage on the East Lancashire Railway pending restoration. Although preliminary work on the restoration of No 752 was undertaken on the Worth Valley, the decision was taken in 2016 to undertake the major work on the East Lancashire Railway with the railway being based there for a ten-year period, albeit allowing for periodic trips across the Pennines. 'Pug' No 19 was displayed statically at the Steamport (Southport) museum until that closed in the early twenty-first century with the collection transferred to Preston as the basis of the Ribble Steam Railway project. In 2020, following completion of the work on No 752, No 19 was transferred temporarily to the East Lancashire Railway for assessing on the viability of restoration to working order; the prognosis was positive and work on its return to steam was completed in early 2022. It was officially launched over the weekend of 18/19 June 2022 when the ELR held an event to mark the centenary of the merger between the LYR and the LNWR. The trust's third locomotive – No 51218 – is currently on static display on the Worth Valley but the trust is looking to see it also restored to an operational condition.

BIBLIOGRAPHY

Bairstow, J.M.; *Railways of Keighley*; Daleman; 1979

Bairstow, Martin; *Keighley & Worth Valley Railway*; Author; 1991

Bairstow, Martin; *The Great Northern Railway in the West Riding*; Author; 1999

Bowling, Mark; *Keighley & Worth Valley Railway through Time*; Amberley Publishing; 2014

Brunt, Paul; *Keighley & Worth Valley Railway Stockbook: A History of the Collection*; KWVRPS; 2013

Chapman, Stephen; *Railway Memories 11: Airedale & Wharfedale*; Bellcode Books; Undated

Collier, David, and Collier, Ben; *The Keighley and Worth Valley Light Railway Through The Years – Part 1 – The 20th Century*; Mainline & Maritime; 2021

Goodall, Mike; *Worth Valley Revival: The Keighley & Worth Valley Light Railway since 1961*; KWVRPS; 1983

Harris, Michael; *Keighley & Worth Valley Railway*; Ian Allan Publishing; 1998

Heavyside, Tom; *Keighley & Worth Valley Locomotives: As They Were*; Midland Publishing; 1996

Higgins, R.; *Worth Valley in Colour: 10 Years of Achievement*; KWVRPS; 1978

Holroyd, John W.; *Worth a Second Glance: A Pictorial Record of the Worth Valley Railway*; KWVRPS; 1972

Huxley, John; *British Railways Past & Present Special: The Keighley & Worth Valley Railway*; Silver Link; 2014

Joy, David; *A Regional History of the Railways of Great Britain: Volume 8 – South and West Yorkshire*; David & Charles; 1975

Povey, R.O.T.; *The History of the Keighley & Worth Valley Railway*; Keighley Railway Society; 1963

Push & Pull

Railway Magazine

Railway World

Whitehead, David; *Worth a Second Glance – Volume 2: A Pictorial Record of the Worth Valley Railway*; KWVRPS; 1981

William, Peter; *Rails in the Worth Valley: A Pictorial Study*; Dalesman; 1973